"Rays of Light"

~ Listen to the Dark

with love...

D1563836

Authored and Channeled by
Linda Street

"Rays of Light"

~ Listen to the Dark

These are channeled teachings from another realm, describing the frequencies of the "Rays of Light."

Authored and channeled by Linda Street

This book was edited for spelling, grammar, and punctuation only by Rev. Debbie Michaels, Penni Dalton, and Pat Percival. Linda channeled all of the content in this book, unless it is specifically indicated otherwise. Linda Street completed any final editing through channeled communication.

"Rays of Light"
~ Listen to the Dark
Authored by
Linda Street

Disclaimer

Linda Street has authored this book with the sole intention and purpose of bringing forth general information to assist others on their paths and in their journeys seeking wisdom and understanding of their physical, mental, spiritual, and emotional growth. The referencing and use of the word *healing* in this book, is meant strictly in terms of how healing is defined within this book. This information is not meant as a medical prescription or medical advice as Linda Street is not a Medical Doctor nor does she dispense or offer medical advisement. This information is not meant to replace the advisement or counsel of any certified professional in the medical community. It is meant to be used in addition to and / or at the recommendation of medical professionals and for those seeking enlightenment. In your choosing to use any of the information offered in this book, you accept sole accountability and responsibility for the outcome, and the author, Linda Street, will assume no responsibility or liability for your choices, your actions, and the outcome.

Dedication

This book is dedicated to every soul, in the past and in the future, that is learning, understanding, and growing on this Earth today. You are all very brave.

To Victoria –
With The highest
Vibration of love.
You are ready to soar.
Please talk to us as we wish
to assist and support you.

Linda Street

"Rays of Light"

~ Listen to the Dark

Authored by
Linda Street
Subject to Copyright © 2014
Contact the author at...
www.healingfromyourheart.com
lindastreet@.healingfromyourheart.com

Acknowledgment

I wish to thank Rev. Debbie Michaels, Penni Dalton, and Pat Percival for their time in editing the spelling, grammar, and punctuation of this book. I thank them also for their feedback and asking good questions that allowed for additional content to be added for a better understanding and interpretation.

I am grateful for my daughter, Andrea Street, in the shooting and preparing of my personal photograph that is used in the book. I also thank my son, Alex Street, for his time in detailing the chakra figures in Chapter 3, to better illustrate the location of the chakras, cones, and grounding cord. Alex also designed my web site for my business. I am grateful for the support of my two children as I grow in my new ventures, even when they may not totally understand them.

Most of all, I am thankful for the assistance of all the Divine and loving beings supporting me each day and in bringing forth this information and these teachings for me to share.

"Rays of Light"

~ Listen to the Dark

Copyright © 2014

ISBN-13: 978-1499330038

ISBN-10: 149933030

Healing From Your Heart, Inc.

Authored By

Linda Street

Contact the author at...

www.healingfromyourheart.com

lindastreet@healingfromyourheart.com

About the Author

Linda Street is an established Spiritual Teacher, Energy Channel, Energy Coach, and Intuitive. Linda accesses the frequencies of the "Rays of Light" to assist in general healing purposes, in the cleansing and re-alignment of chakras, for the purpose of connecting with her guidance, channeled information from another realm, and in sharing that information and the teachings with others.

Linda's past experience in the field of Mental Health and in Human Resources was the perfect path and background to allow Linda to move that knowledge and experience forward into a new world of understanding the metaphysical, and in teaching what she has learned and practiced with frequencies and energies. Linda has added numerous courses and certifications in her field of energy work to her already acquired educational background and experience.

Linda now works exclusively with the frequencies of the "Rays of Light" as she has been gifted with the teachings. She continues to learn, experiment, and practice in using the frequencies and energies as she also shares the frequencies and the information as "teachings" to others. Linda continues to focus on a positive and uplifting approach to assist her and others along their path.

Introduction

Introduction

This introduction is written directly by myself (the author) Linda Street, providing you with a general introduction to the book and its purpose, as well as some interpretation that I feel may assist you as you read. This book is channeled information. Any information that is not channeled, and coming from me as the author, will be specified, just as this introduction is specified as not being channeled.

For clarification, I consider myself a Spiritual Teacher, Energy Channel, Energy Coach, and an Intuitive. I receive intuitive messages, information, and guidance from the Divine realm. With this, I assist myself, and others, in understanding, learning, and creating life solutions, which can all be defined as growth and healing (by the definition in this book.) Through teachings, energy coaching, and energy channeling, individuals are supported in recognizing, understanding, participating, and practicing solutions which allow growth in life and the highest vibrations of love to be supported.

"Rays of Light" – Listen to the Dark is channeled information, channeled directly through myself, as the author. In other words, the information in this book did not come directly from me, but was received by me, through my guides and the Angels in another realm. The information that I received was very specific and also included the titles of the chapters in the book.

The quotations or italics used with various words or phrases in the book are exactly how I received the information in order to highlight the importance. So please view it in that light as you read the material. The italics are for ideas or words where the Angels wanted you to pay special attention to a thought and to highlight its importance. To pause and give it some thought. I was instructed specifically to use quotation marks, for example, in the title "Rays of Light" and in the phrase, "all that is," due to their importance. Of course as the Angels have said, the "Rays of Light" <u>are</u> "all that is."

Several individuals edited the book for spelling, grammar, and punctuation. I reviewed all recommended edits and determined through guidance when additional information or clarification was needed or if an alteration in the wording was acceptable to more accurately relay the information. I received good feedback and questions along with the edits for spelling, grammar, and punctuation. Due to some of those questions, additional information was at times added for more detail to better explain the material or an idea. I am especially grateful for those questions and the feedback that came from the editors.

I physically began writing the book in November, 2013 and began with chapter 6, "Listen to the Dark". This was the chapter that I was asked to write first as I was being taught how to better *hear* the words and information that I was receiving, in order to put it into writing. So I practiced learning how to receive the information, and how to receive it in more detail. I also practiced how to receive the information with more clarity while writing that chapter in particular. The more I practiced, the easier it was to understand and to receive the information. This was especially helpful in completing the rest of the chapters.

You will find that there is a lot of new information in this book and I am being told this information is truth. My understanding is that it is through the writings in this book, the Angels wish to share and teach these truths. I myself found the information to be very interesting as I received it. It was not uncommon for me to lose my place while typing, when a very fascinating piece of information showed up.

For example, those of you that are familiar with chakras will find that in this book there is specific and new information about the primary body chakras and the inter-relationships between them. In this book, your primary body chakras have been described as eight, rather than seven. So please be prepared to read details and information that may not have been introduced to you previously.

The purpose of the book was not to provide all of the answers. The purpose was to provide truth, in information, and to promote good questions to encourage personal exploration. So if you find at the end of the last chapter, that you have more questions than when you started, that has been accomplished. This supports opportunities for growth and healing, and that is the purpose.

You may find the presentation of the material, the style, and the words used to be a little different. Again, this is coming through me, from another realm. So the style and the words are not mine, but coming from beautiful beings. This information is most certainly sent with the vibration of love.

I channeled this book through my heart, and wish to share the teachings and information from my heart to yours. I invite you to live my journey and receive this information through these words, as I encourage you to live your journey, always with the highest vibration of love, joy, and abundance.

Enjoy the teachings. Please use the wisdoms and inspirations to practice, experiment, and to better understand the ways of the universe, allowing your questions to propel you forward in your growth, while you to continue to pursue your truths, bringing true love into your heart and your life.

With Love,

Linda

"Rays of Light"

~ Listen to the Dark

Table of contents

Chapter One
Curiosity of the Rays

Chapter One: Curiosity of the Rays

What is curiosity, if not to illuminate the truth? What are the "Rays of Light," if not to illuminate the curiosity? Light is both curious and at the same time truth. They are one of the same. It is all part of the balance of human life.

"To be or not to be," Shakespeare once wrote. Light or dark, up or down, right or wrong, in or out; one is meant to balance the other. Once you understand "how it works," (how all is meant to be balanced) you have truth and remembrance, struggle to understand and you remain in truth and opportunity. The light will illuminate curiosity and remembrance, while the dark will bring you opportunity. They are both filled with truths. There are always options and you will always have a choice. Which are you choosing at this very moment?

What are your questions about the "Rays of Light?" What sparks your curiosity? What is your reason for picking up this book to read? Did you have to think about it or did you immediately gravitate to the idea? This is attraction at work here. For it is no coincidence that you are now reading these words. You were attracted to the ideas and the information. Or better yet, you were just attracted to pick it up without knowing why, following your attraction with action.

In the following chapters you will be investigating and taking in information and ideas. It will be a little like a detective novel, with the theme unraveling as you read. Your curiosity will take you to the next page and the next chapter and so on. That is the "Rays of Light" at work as not only are they real, they are "all that is." Let this be an introduction.

You are looking for the ending and the answers as you have been doing all your human life. You have been doing so out of patterns, habit, nudging, prodding, maybe responsibility, or obligation. Sometimes you follow the flow and allow the attraction to move you forward.

The power of the "Rays of Light" is ultimate. The "Rays of Light" are "all that is." The "Rays of Light" are a very strong but gentle pull to illuminate and provide the direction that you have been seeking, the answers that you have been so intent on finding. It is like putting the final pieces of the puzzle together or maybe even having those pieces put together for you. That is O.K., for the goal is to understand, not to sweat over it.

Once you have opened this book, and have begun this chapter, you have taken your first step. And a big step that is! It may be perceived as little, but little it is not. You are beginning a journey filled with love and faith. This is faith beyond the imagination. One small step leads to another and another. Before you know it, when you look behind you, you find many giant steps. Yes, you are on your way.

The frequencies of the "Rays of Light" are to assist you on this journey, to lead you, to guide you and to support you. Oh, that you believe, have faith, and trust. This will bring you into the flow of these beautiful frequencies of "all that is," and everything that is perfect for you.

So to begin, let's discuss these frequencies of the "Rays of Light" in a little more detail. It has been stated that the "Rays of Light" represent "all that is." This is very important to understand. Every twitch, every emotion, every action you take and every thought you think are all encompassed in the frequencies of "Rays of Light." They are comprised of every color, every frequency imaginable, and beyond the human imagination, beyond what the human mind can neither fully understand nor imagine. They are filled with beauty and the highest of unconditional love.

Just picture what you would consider a beautiful experience in nature. Visualize yourself standing in the center of that scene taking in every detail of the scents, the beauty, the feelings, and the emotions that this brings. That is but a small sampling of "all that is" in the frequencies of "Rays of Light." It is but a miniscule experience compared to the full experience of the rays.

What is it you wish to experience? What if it were possible for you to choose your experience? What if you were told that you that you could experience whatever you wanted and all you need to do is to dream, to have faith, trust, and believe? Would you be willing to take on this adventure? It will not cost you money, only your time, your intentions and your *will*. Would you be willing to ignite your curiosity and to grab onto the frequencies of the "Rays of Light," and all they represent, and go for a ride? To ride the wave of human life, how it was meant to be, moving with the current and receiving all of the benefits and everything beautiful and perfect for you, rather than the opposite.

Take a closer look at the rays. There are 13 "Rays of Light," coming from the Divine, and each ray represents a unique color and a unique frequency. There are another 258 unique rays, colors, and corresponding frequencies within each of the 13 rays of the Divine. Each of those unique 258 rays, colors, and frequencies, contain another 258 unique rays, colors, and frequencies within each of them. It continues on resulting in an infinite number of unique rays, colors, and frequencies. This may be difficult for the human mind to imagine. So you see it is difficult at best to describe each of these colors and frequencies, and what they represent, as they truly represent "all that is," as they are from the Divine. Also know that each of the infinite "Rays of Light" has a specific Angel assigned to that ray and that frequency. The Angels of the rays bring in information, assist you, and support you each time you access the rays.

So let's look at the 13 "Rays of Light." There are 13 distinct rays, colors, and frequencies, representing the 13 "Rays of Light." Each of those rays is connected and intertwined in a unique way with each of your 13 primary chakras. These chakras will be discussed in detail in Chapter 3. The 8th ray is the ray with the highest frequency, and the one that connects your physical body to "all that is," in the non-physical. The 8th ray encompasses all 13 rays, when this unique connection is sparked, wrapping and securing each ray, allowing them to be interwoven together into a very unique bond with your 8th primary body chakra (your Root chakra,) cementing your physical body together with the non-physical realm and "all that is." That is the best way to describe this in human terms.

This bond, the 8th ray, and your 8th primary body chakra, has a vibration all its own. It is one coming from what can be called your Divine Source. This bond is one that is wrapped in love, colors, frequencies, symbolism, and "all that is." This bond is the highest of all frequencies on this planet and cannot be broken. It is the ultimate *glue* so to speak and is locked in place, just as each color and frequency is locked in place within each ray.

There is significance and symbolism in each of the individual numbers in **258** (the number of rays, colors, and frequencies contained within the 13 "Rays of Light"). This number is also the same number of rays contained in each of those 258 rays, resulting in an infinite number of rays. When you look at each number independently, the **2** corresponds to your connection to the two most powerful frequencies and energies while existing on this planet in your human form, the Divine Source, and Mother Earth. You see, Mother Earth is a living and breathing energy source. This energy source is as important, on this planet, as the frequencies of the

Divine.

The Divine Source of course is "all that is" and is the very powerful source of the frequencies. Together they assist in anchoring you to both this planet Earth and in maintaining your connection to your Divine Source, connecting you to "all that is" through the 13 "Rays of Light."

The number **5** represents the number of your combined primary chakras located above your head and below your feet. Your three chakras above your head are your higher connection you to your Divine Source, while your two chakras below your feet, are your higher connection to Mother Earth. The number **5** and the number **8** added together total 13, representing the 13 "Rays of Light" and your 13 primary chakras.

The number **8** by itself represents your eight primary body chakras. Your 8th primary body chakra (your Root Chakra) is what connects you to your Divine Source and with Mother Earth. This is the chakra that wraps the love, colors, frequencies, symbolism, and "all that is" into the bond that cannot be broken as long as you remain in your physical body. An infinite number of figure eights can been seen interwoven into this bond that cements this beautiful connection.

The 13 "Rays of Light" are here for each of you and you have the choice to accept them or not. You are connected with these rays for sure as that brings you life. However, you also have the ability to consciously access the frequencies of these rays, merely through your intentions. It is you that chooses whether or not to access these rays. You always have choices, and the rays will always be there. When the rays are accepted, they are activated and are cultivated through the actions that you choose. Those actions are associated with your growth, on all levels, and they support and uplift you to move you forward. This assists you in moving into the flow of your physical life in a positive way, rather than struggling against the current, so to speak, and the flow of life.

This does not mean that everything will always go your way or be exactly as you like. Remember there is balance in "all that is." You will need to practice looking at the *whole picture* if you are not already doing that. It is the <u>end</u> of the story, or the result, where you must focus. There will be many twists and turns along the way that may not appear to be what you are seeking. Do not be fooled by this. Sometimes it takes many twists and turns and shifting of the energy to obtain that desired result. There are many lessons for you to learn along your path. The journey allows you the experience and the opportunities to learn and to grow. The end result is the beginning as well as the end. As you focus, your beliefs must always remain true to what you desire in order to bring about that end result that you desire.

Look at the twists with curiosity to bring in light and remembrance. Envision the turns as vehicles and opportunities to take you to your final destination. Above all else, always stay positive and loving in order to enjoy the ride. Always remind yourself that the end is perfect for you. Always intend the end to be of the highest vibration possible and trust that the universe, knowing all of the possibilities, will always bring the best for you, as long as you continue to intend and attract this in your emotions.

What do you wish to attract today? Why not get started. Do you want your day to be positive and uplifting and for example *filled with fun and beautiful surprises?* Why not? Determine that you trust and *know* that will you are experiencing *fun and beautiful surprises* throughout your day. Experience this emotion in the present. Continue to trust and believe. Wake up thinking, living and breathing this experience. Feel and experience the wonderful emotions and the joy throughout the day, as you continue to live and breathe these wonderful feelings.

When you catch yourself experiencing an emotion that does not appear to meet your desire, look at it with curiosity. Say, "Well, I see that is not what I wish to attract, however, I will send love to this experience and this emotion, and know that the ending will be perfect for me. I will watch with curiosity and adventure to see where this goes next. I will notice while continuing to create what I wish with my emotions, and I will stay focused on the ending, and how that will feel. How fun it is to see how I can create. I feel the joy already in my heart. I love fun and beautiful surprises and feel them already."

If you should find yourself experiencing disappointment, which is an emotion with a lower vibration, move away from that, then move right back into the emotions of a high vibration such as *fun and beautiful surprises*. If you do not move away from low vibrations, guess what? You have just changed your creation and intention to one of disappointment, with a lower vibration. Is that what you really wanted to create? Is that how you want to feel, bogged down and heavy with such a low vibration? No, of course not! Move right back into the flow and re-focus on that high vibrating emotion and what you wish to create.

Now this does take practice. You have been living with the same patterns that you have been taught for many years, often times supporting a focus on lower vibrating emotions. There is no judgment here, just recognition of the past and what has been passed along, based on the teachings. It is time to understand that each and every one of your words, thoughts, actions, and gestures is associated with an emotion and a specific vibration. Take a look at this with *curiosity,* which carries a very high vibrating emotion, to illuminate your remembrance of the truth.

You are each deserving of love and understanding, rather than the opposite of struggle and grief. There is nothing to be earned, only that which is to be remembered and understood. Each of you is born of love and each of you is deserving of love. Each of you has a choice, to choose to live with love by living love from the inside, or to choose struggle, and live with the opposite.

So you see, after living with past patterns so long it is like letting go of an old habit and choosing a new one. This takes intentions, love, your will, and practice, and as you do so, you will attract the understanding of how it works. This is where the rays come in. When you are choosing to receive the rays with love and curiosity, you illuminate your path and you are on your way with little steps turning into big steps.

As you put forth your intentions and follow up with your actions and choose high vibrating emotions toward growth, you are met with the assistance of your Divine Source, beautiful Angels, and Archangels, and your guides working with each of the rays and their colors and frequencies of "all that is." Now as it has been discussed there are an infinite number of rays. So you can see there are legions of guides, Angels, and Archangels, or your belief in your Divine Source, just waiting and desiring to assist you with love.

If you should choose to discontinue working on your growth, so be it. That will be supported as well. If you should choose an emotion with a lower vibration, situation, or person, then so be it. The universe will respond just as quickly as you choose and will readily support your choices. There will be more twists and turns. It happens so quickly that you must be very mindful to watch closely as it occurs, so you can understand and learn. Learn how your every thought and your every action is met fully with a response from the universe as everything is kept in perfect balance. Once you understand this relationship, you can begin to see how creation works. You can see how your curiosity and fun, and the attached emotions, can create more of what you want. You can choose to live in the flow, rather than to struggle against the flow, living in the opposite.

Now it is also important to understand that each human being has choices and it is important to respect and understand another's choices. Each human is interconnected in the universe and is one with the Divine Source, and each individual choice has an impact and creates a ripple effect for all others, and the universe.

It is important to be mindful that another's choice that impacts you may not be what it appears at all. You may see it as *bad luck*, "This is not fair," or "This is not right". Remember to look deeper and to trust. Look for the end result.

Understand that you must respect and support others in their *free will* and their choices as well, just as you wish for your free will to be respected and supported. Allow others to choose and experience as you are allowed to choose and experience, without judgment. You each have *free will* and must have respect for your *free will* as well as the *free will* of others. This allows you to attract what is perfect for you, letting go of everything else.

Understand that other's choices may sometimes appear to be hurtful or vengeful to you, but do not be fooled or change your path. Remember those twists and turns that are part of creation. Continue to choose emotions with the highest of vibrations, always, as well as wishing for the highest vibrations for others. Revenge and jealousy are emotions with very low vibrations. Do not be tempted as you will surely steer off course and alter your desired outcome. Stay on course and on your path, with the emotions of high vibrations of love, in order to move you forward, *in the flow*.

The universe sees and knows far more options and opportunities then the human mental mind can begin to imagine. Wouldn't you rather trust in the universe to bring your perfect outcome? Isn't that what you desire, to be happy and joyful and most of all to feel love? Again, remember your part as well in your choice of words, thoughts, actions, and emotions, without judgment.

Be aware, that when following the guidance from your Divine Source, the Angels, or your guides, that you are creating from your etheric (spiritual) heart and this will be different than the habit of following the guidance from your mental mind. You must bring in the emotions of faith and trust and believe in your outcome. It is the final result that must always be your primary focus. What is most important is remaining focused on experiencing the emotions of the perfect outcome. Then watch and learn from the twists and turns and be patient for the outcome. In time, you will learn to better understand this sequence of events and the timing of them.

Remind yourself of the ripple effect that you are creating and how it not only impacts you if you might change your course (with a low vibrating emotion), but most definitely how it impacts all others as well. Remind yourself of what you are attracting at all times. The question is, "Are you attracting what you desire?" Choose what you wish for the outcome. This is a challenge to be curious and to learn to understand how the universe works and how you can receive assistance by choosing to access the illumination in the rays.

The "Rays of Light" are here to stay. They have always been here and will always be. The rays contain frequencies that can be used to cleanse, heal, and balance your bodies. The rays also bring in loving frequencies to assist you with your growth. Your Divine Source, the Angels, and your guides bring in teachings as the rays are packed with information. The rays bring in "all that is" to assist your elevation to the highest vibrating emotions with the vibrations of love and abundance.

You chose to be here and you do not remember as you were born into darkness. You chose to be here and you do not understand as again, you were born into darkness in your physical body. It is time to open up and to receive the "Rays of Light." It is time to not only understand, but to live the "Rays of Light" as they have meaning and bring you love, abundance, and remembrance.

Living with the rays takes on a whole new meaning and a whole new purpose then what has been taught in the past. Your Divine Source, the Angels, and your guides, encompassed in each ray, are here to teach and to assist each of you. This can only be completed with your acceptance and allowance. Your *free will,* will never be violated. You must have full faith and trust.

In order to create the perfect outcome for yourself, you must choose to create where you have not created before. You must desire and put forth the actions to match that desire. Your Divine Source, the Angels, and your guides will provide the guidance as long as you provide the action toward your growth. It is always about growth in this ever changing universe. You must keep up with the growth and be in the flow to truly enjoy your abundance, as the universe will always be changing and flowing.

Now is the time. The time has come to open your hearts and listen, truly listen, to look and truly look, and to hear and truly hear. For it is time for your assignment to unfold. It is time for you to do the unfolding as this cannot be done for you. You are provided what is needed to sharpen your tools, the means, and the assistance. You have always had the tools. The choice is yours. Are you ready?

Chapter Two
Where to Begin

Chapter Two: Where to Begin

As was stated, you were born into darkness. It is time to run from the dark. Yes, it is a balance, of course; however, you are unable to truly live in your abundance when you are walking only in the dark. In order to walk in light, you must allow the rays to assist you in creating balance. Recognize and understand the darkness in comparison. When darkness slips in, bring in the light and the balance.

This will create beauty, love, and a sense of being fulfilled. The frequencies of the "Rays of Light" are your key to bringing you into full awareness of your etheric (spiritual) heart and all it has to offer. Follow this and you will be successful. Choose to stay in the dark and you will struggle, for it is the rays that create the balance. It is you who choose to accept the rays, or not. In choosing the rays and balance you are choosing "all that is." Times are different; your choices will impact you differently. You are now living in a different vibration and it is necessary to allow the "Rays of Light" in order to continue to live in harmony and balance in your physical world.

The time is now, like no other. The time is here and your Divine Source, the Angels, and your guides are here to assist you, just as you have asked. Being born into darkness has clouded and blocked your memory. All memories exist in the frequencies of the "Rays of Light," you see. That is where remembrance lies. As you allow the rays, so you allow the assistance and support. As you allow the rays, so you allow remembrance as they are hand in hand.

But how do you receive the rays? You access them, accept them, and live them. You begin by your allowance. Words, thoughts, actions, and your emotions begin the process. Once you back that up with your actions to support positive growth, the flow begins. You then must pay attention to the guidance, which comes in many forms. It may be obvious or it may be subtle, but it will always be there and it will always be constant.

After sleep walking in the dark for so many years, this may come as a surprise. The new experience, at first, may not feel *normal* to you, but this is normal. This is what was meant to be when stepping into your physical body. It was meant for you to use your etheric (spiritual) heart for the guidance to bring in love and balance and to use your mental mind to keep yourself organized in your physical world. It was never meant for your mental mind to make such decisions for you and to be that guidance. This is where the "Rays of Light" can assist you.

Yes, you are truly not making your own decisions when you allow your mental mind to step in and to decide for you. Many of you are following old patterns and traditions as this is what has been taught for so many years, rather than using your beautiful gifts and listening to your true guidance.

These old patterns have often times taught you to ignore your true guidance and to allow your mental mind to make important decisions. However, your mental mind includes a part of your human body that can be referred to as your ego. Your ego does not have access to information, answers, and true guidance coming from your Divine Source and the Angels. Your ego does not have access to the non-physical world. True guidance can only be accessed by you in understanding how it works and using your etheric (spiritual) heart.

Gathering information and actions for staying organized in this physical world must come from your mental mind. Research, reading, and gathering facts comes from your mental mind, as does putting together charts of comparison and charts for monitoring a business. This is all good information to assist you. You can use your true guidance in directing you as you gather this information. However, when it comes time to actually analyze that information and make decisions and determinations, then it is time to use your etheric (spiritual) heart and ask for assistance and guidance.

As an example, your mental mind can also assist you with keeping your living space organized, laundering your clothing, balancing your checkbook, gathering information to assist you in living in this physical world, and caring for your physical needs, as you do live in a physical world. Your etheric (spiritual) heart can take that information and make an assessment by accessing your true guidance, in order to assist you in choosing, for example, what might be the perfect food for you to eat that is healthy for you and for your best good. You can learn more about foods by taking a course or researching that topic. Then, you must use your etheric (spiritual) heart, "Listen to the Dark"(Chapter 6), and hear the guidance to determine what is best for you, as you are unique, and what is best for you, might not be the same for another.

When you listen to your etheric (spiritual) heart, you hear the answers in the form of true guidance. Gathering the information will keep you organized and focused on the questions that you want answered and the options and choices that you are offered. Listening to your true guidance from your etheric (spiritual) heart provides good answers and direction.

It was meant for you to experience in a physical body what cannot be experienced when your soul is out of your physical body. It was meant for you to learn, to compare, and to grow, always with love from your heart. The universe always allows you to choose, due to your free will; however, those choices have been clouded by blinders, placing you into darkness. Those blinders have kept you from your remembrance of what is beyond your physical world. Those blinders are now removed, and the frequencies of the "Rays of Light" can be accepted, experienced, and used. Now you can see, hear, and feel through your etheric (spiritual) heart without the blinders. The universe can provide your answers and your true guidance when you use your etheric (spiritual) heart.

The blinders are real. You cannot see them in the physical world but you can understand them. They were strapped upon you as you came into the physical world. As human beings you have been *walking in the dark* for many years, not knowing or understanding who you truly are, and not remembering your past. The energy changes and the shifting in your physical world have now removed those blinders. The energy changes have come from your Divine Source and from realms that are currently beyond human understanding. That is change, and now your access to information and answers is more in reach, by using your beautiful gifts, including the "Rays of Light."

Now the time has come for you to know, to know who you are and to understand where you came from and to remember your past. It is time for you to know why you are here, and most of all; it is time for you to understand your purpose and to live your purpose, with happiness and joy in your heart. It is time for you to truly experience and enjoy your life, in a way that has never been experienced before.

Before those blinders were put in place, you are the one who chose to be here in your physical body. You are the one who uses your *free will* to make each and every choice each and every day, for your experience. For life was meant for you to experience and to enjoy, rather than the opposite.

You are the one who decides to allow the rays or not and who chooses to enjoy your life or not. You are the one who chooses your experience. It is truly you who decides when to leave your physical body. Yet, you cannot remember that as you have been living in the dark.

Yes, this may come as a surprise to many of you, but this is truth. The blinders have been removed, yet you may not have noticed. You are used to your old patterns and ways of doing things. However, you can begin to make new choices at this time. You are always making choices; the difference is that your blinders are now off. Do you wish to see truth, or would you rather hide under the covers as if you still have your blinders on? The choice is yours, as always.

The frequencies of the "Rays of Light" can teach you the truth. The frequencies of the "Rays of Light" can show you the truth. But, it is you that must press the start button and take action. It is you that holds the steering wheel for your journey, no one else. There are different ways of course. That is part of your journey, to understand them, and most of all, to practice them in order to fully experience what your heart desires. That is the key. Know them and practice them.....these are the ways.

These ways are the ways of the universe. That is part of "all that is." You do not hold the steering wheel of the *ways of the universe*, yet you <u>do </u>hold the steering wheel for yourself, as you make choices in your physical body. You are the one who steers yourself through your day, and your night for that matter, and through the ways of the universe. You are the one that brightens your day, or not. You are the one who creates your outcomes. You are the one who plants daisies or weeds, and grows and harvests them, and most of all, you are the one who experiences the results.

What to think. This is confusing at first but it will all fall into place once you begin to experience your physical life as it was meant to be experienced. Once you begin to follow your etheric (spiritual) heart for true guidance as was intended and to use your mental mind for organization, as it was intended, you will begin to live *in the flow*.

So you may be asking, what is this etheric (spiritual) heart? Your etheric (spiritual) heart is the true guidance from your Divine Source, the Angels, your guides, and "all that is." Remember, that true guidance can be found in the frequencies of the "Rays of Light." When you chose to come into your physical body, it was understood that you would always have guidance and support available to you. It is not easy to be in a physical body. However, you have made this choice for your experience and growth that can only be attained in this physical world.

The outcome can be astounding and beautiful beyond words. When choosing not follow the guidance and support that was agreed upon, you are choosing to allow and support true chaos in your life that can be likened to a hell on earth. This is not what was meant to be. Life on earth was meant for positive growth and enlightenment. Through your experiences, that life can be shared with others, creating a very brilliant and uplifting ripple effect in this entire universe and beyond. Life on this planet was meant for you to learn and to experience in a physical sense and most of all, to experience the emotions of true love and joy, not the opposite.

Each and every thought, action, and word emitted from each and every human being does in fact create a ripple effect with each soul on this planet and in the entire universe and "all that is." That is the way of the universe. What do you chose to create? Do you choose to create something uplifting and of love, or do you choose to create the opposite? As has been said before, the choice is yours; you have *free will*. Know that you cannot steer the ways of the universe; however, you can choose to steer the choices for yourself.

Now, recognize that it is difficult at best, to steer in the dark. That is why you have your Divine Source, the Angels, and your guides available to you at all times. They are there to shed light on your thoughts, actions, and words, and to allow you to *see* in the dark. The frequencies of the "Rays of Light" illuminate what has been hidden and to assist you with your creations. This illumination allows your soul, within your physical form, to make choices to steer with true light and clarity.

To follow your etheric (spiritual) heart you must listen closely to the guidance and direction being given. You must listen through sight, hearing, using all of your senses, and yes, that includes those little voices in your head. You must listen to the nudges and the little voice on your shoulder, so to speak. As long as those voices are positive and are providing guidance that is not harmful to others, it is true guidance.

You may see words on a billboard, or see something in your mind's eye, experience a dream, hear parts of a conversation, receive a sudden thought (as if a light bulb just went on), experience a *knowing* or *hear* words. It is all guidance. You must practice and learn to recognize the guidance as often times the old patterns have taught you to ignore the guidance or to fear it. The guidance is neither to be ignored nor feared as it is the truth that you have been searching for all these years.

Have you ever suddenly had a feeling of deja'vu as you might call it? This experience is part of the guidance, a little tiny piece of remembrance to be understood as truth to be recognized. A little bit of guidance showing up at just the right moment. Old patterns have often times taught you to ignore this or to rationalize it in your mental mind. That experience of deja'vu would be a truth that is part of your existence, not necessarily from this physical lifetime. It is a remembrance for the purpose of guidance and is meant to be given attention. You must ponder this and ask for additional guidance to remember and understand what this means to you.

You can call upon the "Rays of Light" to allow the frequencies to shed more light on the guidance, to show you the next step or the opportunities that await you. In following this true guidance, you can continue on your path *in the flow* of the frequencies and energies and enjoy the growth experience. Choose to ignore the guidance from your etheric (spiritual) heart and you choose struggle. Again, the choice is yours with your *free will* and the ways of the universe.

Have you found yourself telling yourself what to do? Do not be fooled by your mental mind wanting to make decisions for you. Follow your etheric (spiritual) heart. Allow your true guidance to present itself with all of your options and choices. Then grab on to the steering wheel of your life and begin to steer your ride to your next destination. Your life on Earth is filled with many destinations, stepping from one to the other. Grab onto that steering wheel and do not let go, do not give your precious choices away.

Go with your gut feeling as this is the guidance from your etheric (spiritual) heart. Your gut does not ponder and think about it saying, "Oh, what should I do?" Your gut responds, and responds very quickly. This quick response is true guidance. This must be separated from a quick response driven by a quick temper or judgment that comes from a low vibrating emotion, such as fear or anger. You must practice to learn and understand the difference.

Your etheric (spiritual) heart cannot be seen by your human eye. It is an unseen connection between you and your Divine Source. The connection is in the frequencies of the "Rays of Light" streaming down. Are your channels open and ready to receive? Are you willing and open to receiving? Do you believe that you are deserving of receiving? How do you know if you are unsure whether the guidance is from your etheric (spiritual) heart or your mental mind?

Are you talking to your mental mind and following that guidance? Are you answering yourself, analyzing and saying, "Yes, that seems to be practical" or "I think that would be a good choice?" Did you catch that word, *think?* There is a clue. The etheric (spiritual) heart is not about *thinking.* It is about receiving, and the allowing of the thoughts, information, and emotions to be received and acknowledged, not necessarily in that order.

On the other hand, what did you see or what did you feel and sense? Did you have a snapshot of a word, a vision, or thought come to you? The ideas are given and you are then able to use the steering wheel that has been provided to you, your *free will.* You might say, "But I am very capable of thinking and choosing for myself." It is *I* who does the thinking. Yes, you are the one in your physical body that does make the choice. Your mental mind certainly does the *thinking*. However, true ideas, thoughts, and guidance come from your Divine source, "all that is." This does not take away your *free will* and your ability to choose and make decisions. You are all very powerful creators. However, you are missing the boat to think true ideas come from you, as they truly come to you. Your true power comes from within, in your choices with your *free will* and in how you choose to steer your vessel.

Once you recognize you have full power with this steering wheel and you can truly create, you can clearly see where your power lies. Not in the thoughts and words received, yet in what you choose to do with them. It is then that you can see yourselves as the leader of an orchestra, weaving and spinning, turning, and twisting to direct what you choose to receive and to create. You can see yourself as the Captain of your vessel, steering through the flow of life in waters that may be turbulent and rough at times, however your practice and expertise have taught you how to maneuver into calm waters.

In understanding how this all works, it is truly not work. It is in choosing to steer with consistency, fluidity, love and calmness, and with the highest of vibrating emotions that you begin to create what you desire to receive and experience true enjoyment.

When you put it all together you begin to play a full symphony and experience the beautiful outcome. You can experience the beauty, the love, and the ecstasy that you came here to experience. You can experience the benefits of creating enjoyment. It is as if you were dancing when you do not know how to dance and singing when you do not know how to sing. The result is always beauty, love, and perfection, whether you know how to sing or not, because that is what you have chosen to create.

Let go of what you believe you cannot do and grab ahold of everything that you do believe. Trust that you can and will do it. Use your *free will*. Focus on all that can be done and all that you desire to create and experience. When you open your mouth to sing, only focus on uplifting emotions and that is what you will receive. You need not have the experience, only the desire and the intention and the use of your *will* to choose what is positive and uplifting. This is what creates. That is the way of the universe.

Chapter Three
The Rays and Your Chakras

Chapter Three: The Rays and Your Chakras

Take your time in reading and reviewing this information on your chakras as it is a lot to take in. It may take quite a while before it becomes more familiar to you. That's O.K. Be patient, believe, and trust, and everything will fall into place.

Once you have begun to *let go* and trust you are ready to understand more. Understand that there is more to see, hear, know, feel, taste, notice, and experience. All you need do is to *let go*, truly *let go*, and trust in your Divine Source, the Angels, and your guides. Believe and you will begin the step of truly receiving.

In receiving the frequencies of the "Rays of Light," know that you are receiving "all that is." Then you can begin to work with the rays and all the loving Angels assigned to each of those rays just waiting to assist those who ask. It is that simple. Ask and you shall receive.

Let's take a look at the "Rays of Light" in a traditional simple way. It has been stated that there are 13 Divine "Rays of Light", each ray with a unique frequency, color, and Angel. Each of these 13 Divine "Rays of Light" have 258 rays within them, and another 258 rays within them, resulting in an infinite number of rays, frequencies, colors, and Angels. These colors, the rays, and their *look* are difficult to describe in the physical world. Just as sometimes you might experience beautiful scenery or a beautiful sight, you have difficulty finding words to fully describe to another the full beauty and your experience. So, with that being said, this will be an attempt to best describe with accuracy your chakras, the rays, the frequencies, and their colors.

The 8th ray is the ray with the highest frequency and is one which is very close to your Divine Source, to the universe, and to "all that is." This color is a beautiful purple-violet with a pearl like fluorescent white glow streaming throughout. It represents "all that is" and is forever streaming and flowing, always in motion, just as the universe is always in motion. This ray encompasses and protects "all that is" within all of the rays, the frequencies, and the colors, assisting in cementing together *all*, including the non-physical realm and your physical body.

This frequency is constantly in motion weaving its way in and out and around all other rays and their frequencies, in figure eights, never ending. It seals all of the frequencies as it protects all within them from harm at the time they are being received, which is at all times during your physical life. It carries a force stronger than any other on this planet, yet it is as gentle as a butterfly. This frequency cannot be simulated or reproduced on earth; it can only be produced by the Divine Source, and is received and embedded in each of you within your human body as it connects with your 8th primary body chakra, known as your Root Chakra, and is interwoven within all of your chakras. The 8th ray and your 8th primary body chakra are *one and the same,* so to speak, as they are interwoven and embedded within one another, creating one, and cementing your physical connection with the Divine and "all that is."

Although this highest frequency, the 8th ray, and all of the frequencies are produced only by the Divine, know that you are blessed with this Divine connection and with the ability to access and receive all of the frequencies of the "Rays of Light," on a deeper level, to assist you with your desires. When you access and allow the frequencies of the "Rays of Light," you are more deeply connected on all levels, in the physical and the non-physical. When this is combined with your intentions, opportunities for movement and growth are sparked and stimulated, and you receive Divine assistance.

These frequencies of the "Rays of Light" are meant to work together, in a Divine way, with all the energies, and with all of your Divine chakras. When these frequencies are consciously accessed and accepted by you, and are met with your desire and intention to create, you begin an irreversible process of connecting in a new and unique way with the Divine and with the energies of Mother Earth, deepening your connection to "all that is."

Your Divine Source can be seen or envisioned as God, or your belief in the Divine, including the universe. The Divine includes all Divine beings, and the entire universe and "all that is," which includes you. In receiving the rays, you can choose to move forward with this connection and grow, or you can choose to remain where you are. It is your choice.

Once you have consciously accepted these frequencies, you will always have that choice, from that moment on. That will never change or reverse. Only by your choices will you than choose to create and grow or remain where you are.

If you choose to accept and receive the frequencies of the "Rays of Light" and spark your connection and growth, and you then choose, for example, not to create or to grow at that time, so be it. If at a later time, you decide and say, "Ah, yes, I now see something I did not see before. Yes, I do want to create for myself. I do want to grow and let go of some of the old patterns." At the time when you choose to allow the frequencies and to create and grow, your Divine Source, and the Angels will lovingly work with you, and so your growth continues. If you were again to choose to stop working on your movement forward, so stops your growth, and the deepening of your connection. This is neither good nor bad; it is just your choice.

You need not repeat the conscious acceptance of the frequencies of the "Rays of Light" over and over again to spark this connection as this connection is forever. In consciously receiving the frequencies of the "Rays of Light," this would be able to assist with the cleansing, healing, balancing, and the re-alignment of your chakras. When receiving the "Rays of Light," you can also set a special or specific intention, on a deeper level, if you wish for a *boost*, so to speak. A special intention, for example, could assist you in your releasing and letting go of old patterns, allowing in the higher frequencies, and in making room for patterns that serve you better.

Each time you receive the frequencies of the "Rays of Light" your connection will deepen, you will experience an elevation, and this will allow for your growth. As you continue to accept and allow these frequencies, you will be expanding and growing at a more accelerated rate and the darkness will, over time, slowly begin to dissipate. Your connection will grow stronger and greater and your ability to "Listen to the Dark," (Chapter 6), will become easier as you begin to understand the guidance with greater clarity.

You are always creating. The questions to be asked are: "Are you creating what you want? Are you happy? Are you confident? How do you feel? Are you satisfied? Do you feel joy or are you experiencing the opposite?" It is time to take a close look at this relationship and how your Divine Source can assist you in understanding the universe and how *all* is balanced. Know that what you create is reflected in each of you on a physical, mental, etheric (spiritual), and emotional level, and all levels of the universe beyond and in between.

As stated, the frequencies of the "Rays of Light" can be accessed in order to deepen your connection with your Divine Source, Mother Earth, the Angels, and your guides, and can be used for the purpose of cleansing, healing, and balancing, and for the re-alignment of your chakras, and for receiving guidance, and information. All of the infinite frequencies and colors in the "Rays of Light" coming from Divine Source carry with them the legions of Angels assisting in the movement and flow of the energies and frequencies in an infinite number of ways to exactly where it needs to go. Your Divine Source and the Angels having access and an awareness of "all that is," know exactly where the energies and frequencies need to flow, and where and how they need to be received by you. You need only trust, let go, and accept them.

You can create growth through your intentions while receiving the frequencies and energies simply by intending, in your thoughts or in your words, whatever it is you wish to create and/or release. There is no limit to what you can create. The rays can assist with any situations or relationships that you wish to resolve or attract. But remember, the vibrations that you send out are the vibrations you will attract, and the vibrations are attached to your emotions which are connected to your intentions, words, thoughts, and actions. So if you wish to attract that which is positive and feels good, you must attach very high vibrating emotions to your intentions, words, thoughts, and actions, such as the emotion of love. The emotion of love is the highest vibrating emotion. *Love is the heart of all healing*.

What about those rays and the chakras? Your chakras are your unconscious connection to the "Rays of Light." Your chakras are your connection, through your physical body, to the Divine and "all that is," and to the energies of Mother Earth on all levels; let's take a look at them. There are 13 primary chakras in all, including the 8 primary body chakras, many of which have been introduced to you over the years.

The description of your 8 primary body chakras in this book is a little different from what you may have been previously taught. There are also 3 primary chakras located above your head and 2 primary chakras located below your feet, which makes 13 primary chakras in all.

As you may have noticed there are 13 "Rays of Light" and 13 primary chakras. This is no accident. Each of the 13 rays is connected to one of the 13 primary chakras. Chakra number one is connected to ray number one, etc. The 8th ray is the highest frequency and is connected to your 8th primary body chakra, your Root Chakra. Remember that each of these rays also has an infinite number of frequencies, colors, and Angels.

When life is sparked in a human body, these connections between all your chakras and the rays are created. These connections will remain until your soul leaves your physical body. Further accepting and allowing the frequencies of the "Rays of Light," through your intentions, allow you further opportunities for receiving information, clarity, cleansing, healing, understanding, and growth.

Your 8th primary body chakra, which is your Root Chakra, is all-encompassing. This chakra is your connection to "all that is," and it is interwoven with the 8th ray, which is the highest frequency and the ray of the Divine. This seals together all of the frequencies, energies, and your chakras into your Earthly connection. A beautiful pure golden fountain, filled with the highest of Divine essence on this Earth, can be seen shooting up, out, and into the universe, coming out of a cone above your head. This is your Divine connection, and a reflection of your own Divine essence. **See Figures 3A Primary Chakras, Front View and 3B Primary Chakras, Side View**.

Your chakras can be referred to as *energy centers*, or *processing centers*. Many of you may be familiar with your chakras, but not yet familiar with the chakras located outside of your physical body. There may be many of you that are not yet be familiar with chakras at all. There may also be some of you, familiar with your chakras, but you may be surprised at this description of your chakras in this book. That is O.K. You can learn more about them.

You have many more chakras than the primary chakras that are discussed in this book; however the focus in this book will be on your 13 primary chakras. There is much to learn about each chakra. This will be a discussion on the look and the *mechanics* and some of the primary functions of each chakra related to their relationship with one another and the "Rays of Light." There is infinite interaction and purpose

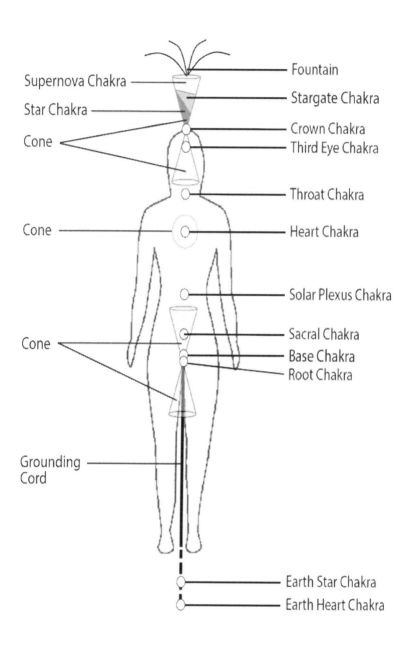

Supernova Chakra

Star Chakra

Cone

Cone

Cone

Grounding
Cord

Fountain

Stargate Chakra

Crown Chakra

Third Eye Chakra

Throat Chakra

Heart Chakra

Solar Plexus Chakra

Sacral Chakra

Base Chakra

Root Chakra

Earth Star Chakra

Earth Heart Chakra

Figure: 3A Primary Chakras, Front View

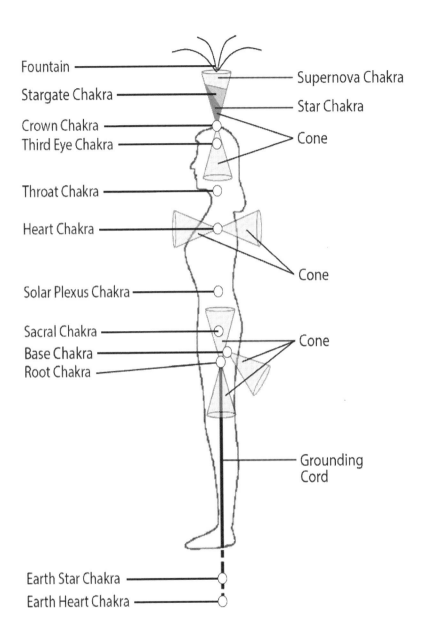

Fountain

Stargate Chakra

Crown Chakra

Third Eye Chakra

Throat Chakra

Heart Chakra

Solar Plexus Chakra

Sacral Chakra

Base Chakra

Root Chakra

Earth Star Chakra

Earth Heart Chakra

Supernova Chakra

Star Chakra

Cone

Cone

Cone

Grounding
Cord

Figure 3B: Primary Chakras, Side View

within and among each of your chakras; the primary inter-relationships of your primary chakras is what will be highlighted.

Your chakras process the frequencies and the energies received by you in your physical body on this the Earth and in the universe. Your chakras also process the frequencies and the energies released and/or directed outward by you, coming from your physical body, out onto the Earth, and out into the universe.

Your chakras are at all times processing frequencies and energies being received and absorbed into your physical body and are processing energies that you release out of your physical body onto this Earth and into the universe. This includes processing all thoughts, intentions, words, actions, and the emotions, with the vibrations attached, coming into your physical body and going out from your physical body.

Everything, yes everything that is energy (and everything is energy, of course), is processed through your chakras, with each chakra having a different purpose and a different function. This would include processing the frequencies of the "Rays of Light," coming from the Divine, and the energies of the Mother Earth, when they are being received and released by you. The vibrations are contained in the emotions carried within both the energies and the frequencies.

As your chakras are processing frequencies and energies, they are coordinating and integrating the interactions and the impact this has on you on a physical, mental, emotional, and etheric (spiritual) level. This is quite a complex and unique connection that works very simply by integrating all with love in a very beautiful and harmonious way. Everything must be in balance and in harmony to function on the most efficient level.

Therefore, it is important for your chakras to be clean and healthy and to be functioning with ease and comfort for you to maintain the perfect balance within your physical body to just plain *feel good* so to speak. Caring for your physical body and your chakras is similar to how you would care for an engine.

You would want to fill an engine with the proper amount of recommended fuel and using the proper amount of recommended oil (changing it at the recommended intervals), cleaning the engine at the recommended intervals and running the engine with care. You would not want to abuse the engine or push it beyond its limits so as to keep it running smoothly and efficiently. Just as an engine, your physical body can take only so much abuse or misuse before your health is impacted. Be aware that your physical body must be properly maintained, to allow your chakras to process with efficiency and for you to just plain *feel good.*

Let's take a look at your primary body chakras. As

mentioned, you have 8 primary body chakras, with the 8th primary body chakra, your Root Chakra, connecting all of your chakras and your physical body to the highest frequency, the 8th frequency, and "all that is," cementing your Earthly and Divine connection. Your 8 primary body chakras are your Crown Chakra, Third Eye Chakra, Throat Chakra, Heart Chakra, Solar Plexus Chakra, Sacral Chakra, Base Chakra, and Root Chakra. They are located within your physical body, hence they referenced as your primary body chakras. **See Figures 3A Primary Chakras, Front View and 3B Primary Chakras, Side View.**

Your primary body chakras appear mostly circular in shape. Each chakra spins with varying degrees of speed. They will also vary in color and will contain varying characteristics, as they each vary in their purpose. Each chakra is permeable, in varying degrees, depending upon their function. Each chakra is also permeable in a different way, related to their unique functions and their unique purpose. They may look similar, but there are distinct differences, depending on the purpose of that chakra. Not all of those differences will be detailed in this book.

As they spin, your Crown Chakra, Heart Chakra, and Root Chakra can be seen with double shaped cones attached, with the points connecting in the center of your chakras. Your Base Chakra can be seen with a single shaped cone, with the point connecting in the center of your chakra. The double shaped cones in your Crown Chakra and Root

Chakra is vertical, with one open end facing upward and the other open end facing downward. The double shaped cones in your Heart Chakra are horizontal, with one open end facing away from the front of your physical body and the other open end facing away from the back of your physical body. The single shaped cone of your Base Chakra can be seen with the open end facing downward, at a 45 degree angle, facing down and away, from the back side of your body.

Your Crown Chakra, Heart Chakra, Base Chakra, and Root Chakra are all spinning, and are circular in appearance; however, the incoming and outgoing frequencies of the Divine essence are what create the appearance of the double and single shaped cones. These cones have a unique function within your physical body. They assist in the receiving and releasing the Divine frequencies and essence, and the energies, and also assist in processing and integrating the Divine frequencies, essences, and the energies, in a unique way.

The frequencies of the Divine essence creating the double shaped cones in your Crown Chakra, Heart Chakra, Root Chakra, and the single shaped cone in your Base Chakra, assist your 8th primary body chakra (your Root Chakra) in your Divine connection to the highest frequency (the 8th ray) and to "all that is." This connection surrounds and fills your physical body in layers of Divine essence, frequencies, and energies, cementing your physical body into the physical world while maintaining your connection to the non-physical realm. These layers can be referred to as your Body Aura, which can be seen as layers of essences, frequencies, energies, and colors of course, all surrounding your physical body. **See Figure 3C Body Aura**.

The single shaped cone in your Base Chakra assists in creating a solid <u>base</u> for all of your primary body chakras, keeping them anchored into your physical body with perfect balance. The purpose of the single shaped cone is for <u>incoming</u> Divine essence and frequencies only, to be integrated with the Earth energies, assisting in the anchoring within your Base Chakra, which creates a very solid base for all of your chakras and your physical body. This base is necessary to assist in supporting your Earthly connection between your Root Chakra and the highest frequency, the 8th ray, and also in creating the perfect balance between your physical body and the non-physical realm.

Your other 4 primary body chakras, your Third Eye Chakra, your Throat Chakra, your Solar Plexus Chakra, and your Sacral Chakra, also appear mostly circular in shape and are spinning, but without the appearance of the cones. At a close examination, some of these chakras will look slightly different in their appearance and in their shape. This is due to their different functions and purpose. It is important for these chakras, as it is for all of your primary body chakras, to be correctly balanced to the same size and to be correctly aligned within your physical body.

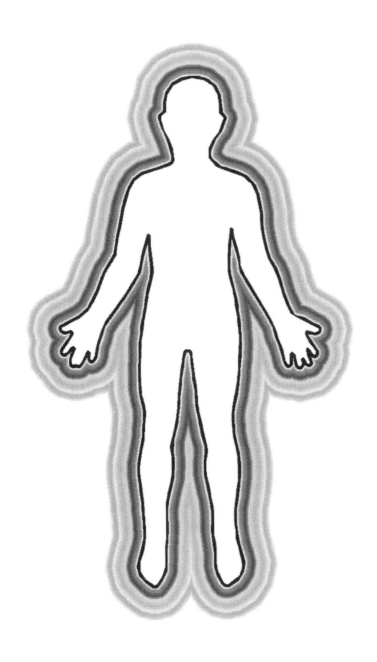

Figure 3C Body Aura

The appearances of your 3 primary chakras that are located above your Crown Chakra look different than any other primary chakras in their appearance. They are called your Supernova, your Stargate, and your Star Chakras. They are spinning, however, they are the only chakras that each take on the shape of the cone above your Crown Chakra, rather than being mostly circular in shape. They are your gateway and your connection to the Divine, your Divine Source as you know it. They <u>are</u> Divine. **See <u>Figures 3A Primary Chakras, Front View and 3B Primary Chakras, Side View</u>.**

Your Supernova Chakra, Stargate Chakra, and Star Chakras interact with all of your primary chakras, within your physical body and outside of your physical body, and specifically assist in the receiving of the frequencies of the "Rays of Light." The primary purpose of these three chakras is to attract and to usher in the frequencies of the Divine and the Divine essences. They also assist and support the connection between your 8th primary body chakra (your Root Chakra) and the 8th ray.

The 3 primary chakras above your Crown Chakra also assist in the integration of the energies of Mother Earth with the Divine essences and the frequencies of the "Rays of Light," for your experiences and growth. It is all about your experiences and growth. These chakras also have a unique relationship with your Heart chakra, assisting your Heart Chakra in directly receiving the frequencies of the Divine and "all that is" and your pure connection to truth, love, and remembrance.

Your 2 primary chakras located below your feet, your Earth Star and your Earth Heart Chakras, are circular in shape and assist with your Divine connection to Mother Earth. These chakras are very important in the receiving of the Earth energies and pushing them up into your physical body to join with the frequencies of the Divine. These chakras assist in your being balanced and staying grounded and rooted into the Earth, in a physical sense, allowing you clarity and understanding in your physical world.

Each of your chakras deserves some specific attention. Following are more details regarding your primary chakras. Again, this information is sometimes difficult to describe in a physical sense, so this is an attempt to best describe your chakras with the most accuracy.

Your Supernova Chakra can be considered your 11th primary chakra and assists with your connection to "all that is," assisting in linking you to your 8th body chakra and the highest frequency (the 8th ray) that is *all encompassing*. This chakra sits the highest of the chakras above your head and can be seen near the top of the open end of the cone above your Crown Chakra. This chakra is intertwined with your Stargate Chakra and Star Chakra in a particular way as it assists in bringing the frequencies of the Divine essence into your Crown Chakra and all of your primary chakras.

A beautiful violet-purple essence can be seen on the <u>outside</u>

of this cone, surrounding and swirling in a downward motion, going into the cone, downward towards the point of the cone and into your Crown Chakra. This chakra and its Divine essence assist in forming the shape of the cone and as it is intertwined with your Star Chakra and your Stargate Chakra in a particular way. As the Divine essence swirls downward past the point of the cone and into your physical body it makes a special connection with your Heart Chakra, as it simultaneously interlocks with each of your primary body chakras.

The violet-purple Divine essence in your Supernova Chakra begins at the top, on the <u>outside</u> of the cone, the open end of the cone. As this essence moves downward, it transforms, while integrating and dissolving into the colors of the other 2 chakras above your Crown Chakra (each of these colors will be reviewed next) spiraling and swirling downward and descending into the point of the cone.

A beautiful Divine essence can be seen coming out of the top of the Supernova Chakra shooting upward and out from the <u>inside</u> of the open end of the cone. **See <u>Figures 3A Primary Chakras, Front View and 3B Primary Chakras, Side View</u>**. This glorious fountain can be seen spraying a beautiful electric and bright golden hue, with the added essence of a fluorescent pearl white, shooting up from the center of your Crown Chakra, through the center of the cone, and out of the top of the cone. This spray dissipates into of beautiful white essence, the purest of white, a truly Divine essence as it dissipates up and out and into the universe. This fountain is a reflection of your Divine essence, your soul, and who you really are outside of your physical body.

Your Stargate Chakra can be considered your 10th primary chakra and also assists with your connection to "all that is," assisting in linking you to your 8th body chakra and the highest frequency that is "all encompassing." This chakra is intertwined with your Supernova Chakra and your Star Chakra in a particular way as it assists in bringing the Divine essence into your Crown Chakra and into all of your primary body chakras.

This chakra can be seen above your Crown Chakra, and below your Supernova Chakra, swirling around predominantly to one side (the side can vary) on the outside of the cone, blending with your Star Chakra and the Divine essence to form the shape of the cone. The swirl of your Stargate Chakra is sideways and swirling downward as it blends with your Star Chakra coming around the cone from the opposite side, swirling down towards the point of the cone and into your Crown Chakra and into your physical body.

The colors of your Stargate Chakra are not human color; it is similar to a bronze color on the golden side. There is a connection and there are sparks, as the essence of this chakra rubs up against the essence of your Star Chakra. Both the Star and the Stargate Chakras are spinning, swirling, combining, and sharing colors, frequencies, and energies, as the two chakras swirl downward and into your Crown Chakra. At times, it is difficult to differentiate between your Stargate and your Star Chakras. The best way to differentiate is that one chakra can be seen swirling predominately on one side of the cone, while the other can be seen swirling predominantly on the other side of the cone, each with their unique colors.

Your Star Chakra can be considered your 9th primary chakra and also assists with your connection to "all that is," assisting in linking you to your 8th body chakra and the highest frequency that is *all encompassing*. This chakra is intertwined with your Supernova Chakra and your Stargate Chakra in a particular way as it assists in bringing the Divine essence into your Crown Chakra and all of your primary chakras.

This chakra can be seen above your Crown Chakra, and below your Supernova Chakra, swirling around predominantly to one side (the side can vary,) on the outside of the cone, blending with your Stargate Chakra and Divine essence to form the shape of the cone. The swirl of your Star Chakra is sideways and swirling downward as it blends with your Stargate Chakra coming around the cone from the opposite side, down towards the point of the cone and into your physical body.

The colors of your Star Chakra are not human colors. The

Star Chakra can be seen as a violet turning into a beautiful hue of golden blue, with a hint of electric yellow. There is a connection and there are sparks, as the essence of this chakra rubs up against the essence of your Stargate Chakra, spinning, combining, and sharing colors, frequencies, and energies, as the two chakras swirl downward and into your Crown Chakra. At times it is difficult to differentiate between your Star and your Stargate Chakras. The best way to differentiate is that one chakra is swirling predominately on one side of the cone, while the other is swirling predominantly on the other side of the cone, each with their unique colors.

Your primary body chakras have been discussed and described by many over thousands of years. This is a description of the *mechanics* of what can be seen and understood of your 8 primary body chakras, the 8th ray, and the inter-relationship between your primary chakras and how they relate to the frequencies of "Rays of Light" and the energies of Mother Earth.

All of your chakras work very closely together and have special and unique relationships between and among them as they process the frequencies from the Divine, the human energies, and the energies of Mother Earth. The chakra's locations of your primary body chakras are approximate, and can vary slightly depending on the size and shape of each individual person's physical body.

Your Crown Chakra, Third Eye Chakra, Throat Chakra, and Heart Chakra can be considered your upper body chakras and spin faster than your lower chakras. Your upper chakras all spin at a similar rate. Your Solar Plexus Chakra, Sacral Chakra, Base Chakra, and Root Chakras can be considered your lower Chakras and each of them spin at a progressively slower rate than your upper chakras. They spin progressively slower, beginning with your Solar Plexus Chakra going downward toward your Root Chakra.

What is considered your 7th primary body chakra is called your Crown Chakra and is located at the top of your head. This chakra is circular in shape and is swirling and spinning at the top of your head as it assists in guiding the Divine essences into your physical body and into all of your primary body chakras.

Both open ends of the cones in your Crown Chakra are your etheric connection, between your primary body chakras, your chakras above your Crown Chakra, and the Divine essences and frequencies. The Divine essences within your Novastar Chakra, Stargate Chakra, and your Star Chakra assist in creating the shape of the upper cone. The Divine essences alone create the shape of the lower cone.

Your Crown Chakra also assists with your Divine connection to "all that is," guiding the Divine frequencies and essences down into your primary body chakras and into your physical body. All Divine essences and frequencies enter your physical body through your Crown Chakra and simultaneously interlock with each of your primary body chakras. All Earth energies enter your physical body through your Root Chakra. The combining of the Divine essences and frequencies with the Earth energies, when they intermingled within your Root Chakra, is what truly sparks your Divine connection between the highest frequency (the 8th ray) and your Root Chakra (your 8th chakra), creating and maintaining your existence within your physical body. This connection is what also creates your Body Aura, surrounding you in layers of essences, frequencies, energies, and colors.

There is a unique connection between your Crown Chakra and your other upper chakras; your Third Eye Chakra, Throat Chakra, and Heart Chakras. Your Crown Chakra assists in the integration of the essences, frequencies, and energies between all of the upper chakras in particular, and in your communications through each of these chakras. This is true for whether you might be giving or receiving vibrations and would also include the processing and receiving of your Divine guidance.

Your Crown Chakra is a pure white, yet a different color of white that is seen in the pure white of the Divine essence dissipating from the fountain in the center of your Supernova Chakra. This white is quite brilliant and fluorescent and can be considered a reflection of Divine Essence.

What is considered the 6th chakra is known as your Third Eye Chakra, and can also be referred to as your Brow Chakra. This chakra is located between and slightly above your two brows. This chakra brings in, processes (translates), and integrates, information from another realm to assist you with your intuition, your gut feelings, your inspirations, guidance, information, and inspirations being received from the Divine.

This chakra assists your Heart Chakra specifically by processing and integrating information and essence received from the Divine realm, and through the Divine connection with your chakras located above your Crown Chakra. Your Third Eye Chakra processes and integrates this information and essence as it travels down from your Crown Chakra, into your Third Eye Chakra, transitioning through to your Throat Chakra, and flowing downward into your Heart Chakra.

This integration is important for bringing forth clarity in truth, specifically the recognition of truth, as it assists you in your growth. The information, revelations, and inspirations may manifest directly in your Heart Chakra or it may transition to another primary body chakra for manifestation.

This chakra is circular in shape and is a very beautiful and brilliant, electric indigo blue in color that can be seen swirling between your brows. Sometimes it can be seen as florescent, flat, or even a pale white depending on the energies and frequencies that are being received and integrated.

What is considered your 5th chakra is known as your Throat Chakra and is located in the center of your throat. This chakra is circular in shape and assists in processing of frequencies and energies specifically related to your communication, in all forms.

The frequencies are received from the chakras above your Crown Chakra, processed through your Crown Chakra, your Third Eye Chakra, your Throat Chakra, and next transitioned to your Heart Chakra. The frequencies are integrated and intertwined with the essences and energies of your Heart Chakra, while at the same time integrated and intertwined with the essences and energies of your Third Eye Chakra. Together, these frequencies, essences, and energies are integrated and processed back through to your Throat Chakra to assist in your communication. This communication involves the processing the vibrations of the energies in all of your words, thoughts, and actions.

The interactions of the essences and the energies are taking place between your Crown, Third Eye, Throat, and your Heart Chakra (your etheric or spiritual heart) to assist your Throat Chakra with communication. There is a very special connection taking place between your Heart Chakra and your Throat Chakra at this time. Your Throat Chakra receives and transmits the communication in the form of your words, thoughts, and actions in a physical sense (ie. your spoken words, thoughts, or your actions), while your Heart Chakra simultaneously receives and transmits these same communications in the form of the vibrations of your emotions in a non-physical sense. You will better see how this works in the discussion about your Heart Chakra.

Your Throat Chakra can be seen as a light colored powder blue, very soft, softened by a beautiful gentle shade of white, and yet a different white from the white essence in your Crown Chakra and the white essence dissipating from the fountain in your Supernova Chakra. The swirling motion of this chakra shows the layers of softness of the white mixing and combining with the essence of blue, to create a beautiful and very soft blue essence, with only a very slight amount of fluorescence to be seen swirling within the layering of the blue and white.

What is considered the 4th chakra is known as your Heart Chakra and is located in the center of all your primary body chakras. This chakra is circular in shape and receives the frequencies from the rays from the Divine realm, coming through your Crown Chakra (directly and indirectly), and the energies of the Earth coming through your Root Chakra.

These frequencies can be translated, processed, and integrated both directly from the Crown Chakra, and with the assistance of your other primary body chakras. Your Heart Chakra also has a very special connection to your

Throat Chakra, in receiving, processing, and transmitting the vibrations attached to your emotions as they are created and received. It is your Heart Chakra that receives and transmits the vibrations within your thoughts, words, and actions in the non-physical out into the universe, which will in turn attract back the same vibrations.

The Divine essence of your Heart Chakra forms two cones with their points located in the center of the chakra. These essences assist in the linking of your 8th body, your Root Chakra, with the 8th ray, the highest frequency. Both open ends of the cones in your Heart Chakra assist in your etheric connection to the Divine and the Divine frequencies.

The open end of the cone in your Heart Chakra extending to the front side of your physical body, also serves to translate, transmit, and send out energies in the form of vibrations, through your intentions, thoughts, and words, towards others, and out into the universe, into the non-physical realm. These are the same vibrations that are attached to your emotions that have been transmitted in a physical sense through your Throat Chakra in that special relationship. The vibrations are created by you, within your emotions that are attached to situations, objects, and other persons, and in your words, thoughts, and actions, and are transmitted out into the universe as they leave through the front of your Heart Chakra, moving with speed and the accuracy of radar, guiding and directing them as to where they are to be received.

The open end of the cone extending to the back side of your physical body serves to receive and translate the energies in the form of vibrations, as they are received by you, as you attract back to you the exact <u>same</u> vibrations through the emotions that you sent out from the open end of the cone extending to the front of your Heart Chakra. These are the matching vibrations that were processed through a special connection with your Throat Chakra, and the matching vibrations that were sent from your Throat Chakra and the front of your Heart Chakra. Everything must be in balance.

Therefore, the exact vibrations, attached to your emotions, that you have intended and sent out through the front of your Heart Chakra, are attracted right back, and received through the cone in the back side of your Heart Chakra. This is, in part, why it is not so readily recognized that you are creating what you attract, as it sneaks in the back door, so to speak, the back side of your Heart Chakra. But make no mistake; these vibrations will always be balanced.

Your Heart Chakra is located in the center of your chest and is filled with beautiful and varying shades of green, intertwining and swirling with a bit of an electric pink color and a small bit of streaming white essence as a reflection of the Divine. The greens can be brilliant or flat but the electric pink is always brilliant and fluorescent in color. The Divine essence in this chakra is what forms the shape of the cones, each extending from the center of your Heart Chakra, towards the front and towards the back of your physical body.

What is considered the 3rd chakra is known as your Solar Plexus Chakra and is located approximately 2-3 inches above your naval. It is sometimes oval as it spins and whirrs ever changing between oval and circular in its shape, yet very deliberate and exact with its inconsistency. The spinning of this chakra is slightly slower than your Heart Chakra.

Your Solar Plexus Chakra is interconnected with all of your primary chakras in a very unique way. There are multiple layers of essences in and around this chakra at all times. This chakra assists all of your primary chakras by its cleansing, processing, and integrating of the Earth energies and the processing and integrating of the frequencies of the "Rays of Light" with the Earth energies. This cleansing, processing, and integration process is related to your soul, and your growth, as it impacts you on a physical and non-physical level. This process includes the Divine frequencies, along with the information, that is being received, integrated, and processed through your Crown Chakra, and the energies received from the Earth that are processed through your Root Chakra, as it is all related to your growth.

There is a need for a slower spin in this chakra to ensure a balance in the integration process. It has many unique characteristics and is permeable, in every way. It is permeable, acting as a filter, to assist in the releasing of your old patterns and the integration of your new growth. It is the essence of the Divine that assists this chakra with the integration of your growth.

This chakra can be seen as a bright golden yellow. It is gleaming, swirling, and is quite brilliant, intertwined with a very beautiful soft shade of pearl white surrounding the edge, similar to the white in your Throat Chakra, and can be likened to a beautifully glowing sun that you might see against a deep blue sky. The circular/oval shape of your Solar Plexus Chakra is ever changing but this is deliberate and with purpose.

What is considered the 2nd chakra is known as your Sacral Chakra and is located just below your naval. Your Sacral Chakra is circular in shape and assists your Solar Plexus Chakra in filtering the energies of the Earth and integrating them with the frequencies of the Divine. The energies are filtered in the Sacral Chakra as they are received from your Root Chakra, and travel up to your Solar Plexus Chakra for absorption, filtering, and integration. This chakra is continuously pushing the energies to assist in the filtering of these energies. The level of filtering in this chakra is great; therefore there is a need to spin at a slower rate than your Solar Plexus Chakra in order to maintain the perfect balance.

The color of your Sacral Chakra is a glowing orange, similar to the color of a brilliant yet soft and lovely glowing sunset. It can be seen as the purest of orange with the shimmer of yellow around the edges (sometimes appearing brown in color) and surrounded by a soft white glow, allowing its brilliance to clearly be seen.

What is considered your 1st chakra is known as your Base Chakra, which is located, cradled just above the base of your spinal cord, slightly towards the back of your spine and your physical body. This chakra is slightly above and behind your Root Chakra, sometimes so close to that chakra, that the two may be touching. It is slightly off center from the other primary body chakras due to its function. As your connection to the Divine and to Mother Earth deepens, and is elevated, there slowly becomes a greater separation of space between your Base Chakra and your Root Chakra.

Your Base Chakra is circular in shape and has a unique relationship with your Root Chakra. The primary purpose is to provide a secure and solid base, in order to anchor all of your primary body chakras into your physical body, bringing you continuity and balance. Your Base Chakra also supports balance during the integration and processing of the Divine essence, the frequencies, and the energies within and between all of your primary chakras inside and outside of your physical body.

Your Base Chakra functions together and separately with your Root Chakra. This chakra receives assistance from your Root Chakra in anchoring your physical body into Mother Earth and in the receiving of Earth energies, to assist with this chakra's primary purpose. Your Base Chakra is spinning at yet a slower rate than your Sacral Chakra.

The single shaped cone with its point in the center of your Base Chakra is tilted at an angle with its open end facing somewhat downward, towards the back of your physical body, at about a 45 degree angle. This cone serves to only receive the Divine essence to assist in its primary function and in maintaining a solid base for your balance.

This chakra can be seen as very dull and very deep, dark red in color, without the brilliance or the fluorescent that can be seen in other chakras. The dull red begins to lighten slightly toward the outer edges. A very light dull pink, then a dull medium brown color can be seen on the outside edges of this chakra. A small amount of a dull white color, a reflection of the Divine, can be seen intermittently interlocking and swirling between these colors. The dullness in the coloring serves as a very dense and heavy and solid base to assist with its unique functions, hence the very slow spin to this chakra.

What is considered your 8th chakra is known as your Root Chakra. Your Root Chakra is your Divine connection with the highest frequency, the 8th ray, bringing your entire physical body into harmony and balance with the Earth, the physical world, and the non-physical realm. Your Root Chakra anchors you into the inner core of the Earth, with a deep rooted connection, intertwining the Earth energies with the essence of the Divine, the frequencies of all of the "Rays of Light," and "all that is." This connection gives you life. Once this connection is broken, your soul can no longer remain in your physical body.

Your Root Chakra can vary from person to person in exactly where it is located. It typically sits close to your Base Chakra, slightly below and in front of that chakra, about 2 inches below the tip of your spine. Your Root Chakra is spinning at yet a slower rate than your Base Chakra as it assists in attracting, absorbing, filtering, and elevating the energies of Mother Earth from your primary chakras below your feet. As your connection to the Divine and Mother Earth deepens and becomes more elevated, there slowly becomes more separation of space between your Base Chakra and your Root Chakra.

Your Root chakra has a very special connection with your Base Chakra, as it assists with the integration of the Earth energies and in sharing the deep rooted energies with your Base Chakra. This is most important in supporting the primary function of the Base Chakra.

The Divine essence of your Root Chakra forms two cones with their points located in the center of the chakra. It is the essence of the Divine that that forms the shape of the cones. The open ends of the cones in your Root Chakra assist in your etheric connection to the Divine frequencies of the "Rays of Light" and "all that is," the Earth energies, and the connection with the 8th ray (the highest frequency). This connection is permanent as long as you remain in your physical body. This is your Divine connection that gives you life as you know it in your physical body.

The cone with the open end facing upwards, towards your Divine connection above your Crown Chakra, is assisting in the receiving of the Divine essence, the frequencies, and in the filtering and intermingling of these frequencies with the Earth energies in your Root Chakra, Earth Star Chakra, and your Earth Heart Chakra. Your Root Chakra exchanges the Divine essence, frequencies, and the Earth energies, between and among all of your primary chakras, including the chakras above your Crown Chakra.

Through this chakra and this cone, there is an interlocking of the Earth energies with the Divine essence, as they are being absorbed, filtered, processed, and transmitted through all of your primary chakras, including your Divine connection. This process is like clockwork, without interruption. The filtering in this chakra is a different type of filtering that occurs in your Solar Plexus Chakra. Your Root Chakra specifically filters the Earth energies.

The cone with the open end facing downward, towards your two primary chakras located below your feet (your Earth Star and Earth Heart Chakras), assists in the process of attracting and absorbing the Earth energies to be processed and filtered up through all of your primary body chakras. It assists in solidly grounding and anchoring you deep into the physical plane, into the core of Mother Earth, and in being deep rooted into the physical world. This is for the purpose of staying grounded and balanced when integrating with the Divine and the high frequencies of the "Rays of Light." This will assist you with your clarity and understanding in your physical world.

This connection can be deepened and elevated over time as you continue to access the frequencies of the "Rays of Light," anchoring you more deeply into the physical, strengthening your connection to Mother Earth, allowing you greater enlightenment. The deepening of this connection occurs simultaneously with the elevating of your connection to the Divine and the higher frequencies, as all must be in balance, always.

Your Root Chakra is circular in shape and can be seen as a multitude of very deep, dull, and dense shades of brown. There is no fluorescence or brilliance, however, the flat, white essence of the Divine can clearly be seen intermingled within the shades of brown. The colors are deep and dense to support its purpose; hence this is the chakra that spins the slowest of all of the primary body chakras. However, with the assistance of the frequencies the spin may be slow, but it is very consistent, running like clockwork.

Next is a discussion of your primary chakras located below your feet. These chakras are your greatest connection to Mother Earth and the Earth energies.

What is considered the 12th chakra is known as your Earth Star Chakra, and is located below your Root Chakra, and below your feet. It spins at a slow rate, slower than your Root Chakra, however the spin is very different in this chakra. As this chakra spins, it turns ever so slightly rotating the direction of the spin, with perfect consistency, maintaining the exact same number of rotations per minute.

Your Earth Star Chakra is located outside of your physical body, and below your feet, to assist in a very deep rooted connection of your physical body, Mother Earth, and the Earth energies. It is circular in shape and it does not take the shape of the cone below your Root Chakra. This chakra has a unique bond with your Root Chakra and a purpose to assist your physical body in staying *grounded* and maintaining clarity while you are receiving high level frequencies from the Divine.

This chakra also assists in the filtering process with the Earth energies that can become very heavy from the absorption of low vibrations, hence the very slow rate of its spin. Mother Earth very readily absorbs low vibrations from human beings, situations, and objects to assist you in keeping your body healthy on all levels, therefore the low vibrations that are absorbed into the Earth must be filtered out.

This chakra is mostly the color of dull copper with a very slight shimmer to it. It contains some hues of gold and brown with a slight bit of a dull white streaming within the circular motion of the chakra as it turns.

What is considered the 13th chakra is known as your Earth Heart Chakra and is located below your Earth Star Chakra. This chakra is your greatest Divine connection to Mother Earth, as it is the heart of Mother Earth. This chakra spins at a very slow rate, slower than the Earth Star Chakra, however this spin is also very different than in the other chakras.

As this chakra spins, it turns ever so slightly rotating the direction of the spin, with perfect consistency, maintaining the exact same number of rotations per minute. This chakra is also changing to an imperfect shape while it spins, taking on the appearance of being mostly circular, while pumping ever so slightly and moving ever so slowly, similar to the way that a human heart would look as it is beating and pumping, except at a much slower rate.

Mother Earth is pumping her beautiful and very powerful energies through this chakra and into your other primary chakras to assist in the perfect balance of your body on all levels, in the physical and non-physical. This is the chakra that has the primary responsibility for bringing in that connection of the energies of Mother Earth into your physical body. This Chakra assists in completing your Divine Earthly connection.

This chakra contains the color of a very deep and dull dark green, with hints of brown and copper. There is no florescent or shimmer to this color, just a very dull, deep, and dark in color. There is an ever so slight hint of soft flat white essence that can be seen in between pumps, as a reflection of the Divine.

Your Grounding Cord is created within your Root Chakra, beginning in the center, and extending downward into the Earth. The Earth energies, your Earth Star Chakra, and your Earth Heart Chakra assist in the extension of this cord downward into the earth. This connection is solid and assists the Root Chakra in your deep rooted connection, and in solidly grounded into the Earth.

Your grounding cord will become wider and will begin to extend deeper into the Earth as you *elevate your divine connection* and become more deeply rooted into the physical, deepening your connection to both the Divine and Earth energies. This occurs little by little, over time, as you continue to access the "Rays of Light." The solid line going downward from your Root Chakra in **Figures 3A Primary Chakras, Front View and 3B Primary Chakras, Side View,** indicates your natural grounding cord at your time of birth. The dotted lines where the grounding cord goes beyond the surface of the Earth, and into Mother Earth, indicate your possibilities to further deepen your connection with the Earth energies.

Chapter Four
Go to the Light

Chapter Four: Go to the Light

What first comes to your mind when reading this title, "Go to the Light?" Do you feel light, in the sense of energy lightness? Do you see, sense, or feel physical light? Are you feeling drawn to what has been proposed to you? This is a good example of *how it works*. What was your fist thought or your first visual? Did you picture the flicker of a light or experience the feeling of lightness? You see the art of suggestion is more than suggestion, it is real. If you focus on the premise, as a given, then you can see how easy it can be to create, and create you will.

Will is an interesting word to consider. What is it that you *will* to create? Your *will* is part of the formula to creating. Your free *will* allows you the freedom to create. It begins with a thought, a word, or a visual in your mind. You immediately attach an emotion to that. Next, your belief, your trust, and your *will* bring your creation to fruition and carry it forward.

An idea or thought may appear to start out in your mental mind but can easily move to your etheric (spiritual) heart if you so desire. However, you truly create directly from your Divine Source and through your etheric (spiritual) heart.

So let's say that you wish to create more acceptances from others. It begins with you and your thoughts and desires, and with your emotions that are attached to them. Do you accept that you are worthy of this acceptance and believe it in your heart? Notice the emotion that is attached to those thoughts and your beliefs. Do you feel unsure? Do you say to yourself, "Yes, but I am not perfect or deserving." Notice the low vibrating emotion of doubt that is attached to that thought.

Learn to use your *will* to create the reflection of others believing in you as you learn to believe in yourself, from your etheric (spiritual) heart. Attach high vibrating emotions in knowing you are deserving of love and acceptance. Confidence is a very high vibrating emotion. Fill your emotions with the vibrations of love and belief to bring in your emotion of confidence. Do not stray from that focus and those emotions or you will bring in different emotions and will create something different. Continue to *go to the light*, and your *will*, so to speak, will be done. Stray, and your *will*, so to speak, will again be done.

You see everything starts with you. You are here to create, and create you will. Your focus will always start with you. Let us say that the *light* is your focus. Included in that focus, or that *light*, is your intention, "I am accepted." Attach very high vibrating emotions to those thoughts and words. Use your *will* to carry it forward. Experience the emotion of acceptance in your heart and let go of all else, truly let it go. Believe and trust in yourself, and know that you are accepted. Anything else is false.

Be aware of trickery. You may notice an experience that

suggests something different to you. You may feel that a certain behavior from another is not accepting of you. Do not fall into the trap of believing anything different from your original and true focus and high vibrating emotions. Follow your etheric (spiritual) heart and your true desires; that is all that matters. Let go of any judgment of others. Stay focused on your intention and your high vibrating emotions until you have attracted and are experiencing the perfect outcome. Be patient through to the end.

If you begin to experience a perception of a *road block*, do not fall into that trap for that is trickery. Remember, you create what you wish, or *will*. If you were to believe in that *road block*, and as a result, you experience that low vibrating emotion of defeat or loss, then that *road block* will become your new creation. Remind yourself to stay focused on your intention and the emotions that you desire. *Go to the light* until you have moved past a perceived *road block* and continue to attract that which you wish to create and experience. You must have patience and trust and continue to believe until you have reached your desired outcome. Know this with trust and confidence.

Remember that there are many others who are creating just as you are. Remember other persons, along with their Divine Source, the Angels, and their guides are all working with the frequencies and the energies to create as well. Some creations may take place very quickly and some may take more time. Each intention, with its emotions, is unique, just as you are unique, and will come to fruition at the perfect time. You will begin to notice just how perfect it is as you notice and understand more and more how you create.

Be very aware of your emotion attached to your intention. Look at it very closely and ask yourself, "Is this truly what I want to create?" In other words, be careful that what you are asking for is exactly what you want. Look carefully at your words and thoughts, as one word or thought can bring in a different emotion and can make a difference in the outcome. Notice how the emotion *feels* to you. What you are wishing to create and the emotions that are attached to that thought or idea may be two very different things. Does the emotion feel light and uplifting or does it feel heavy and drag you down?

Notice that you automatically attach an emotion to each one of your thoughts, words, and intentions, and in doing so you are emitting a vibration. Those vibrations attract the same vibrations right back to you, as a reflection and a balance. So each time you attach that vibration to your emotions, you must be aware and know that you are attracting back the exact same vibration with the same intensity of that emotion.

As an example, when you put out to the universe a vibration of anger, you may or may not attract anger directly back to you. You will be attracting that vibration with the same intensity of the emotion that is attached; however, the vibration reflected back to you can take many different forms. Other such forms may be hate, retaliation, jealousy, or judgment, which can be experienced in different ways, with different persons. The vibration is the same even though the resulting experience may be different. Be very aware that these vibrations are without a doubt related, and that it is your attraction and it is the result of what you have created. Remember, everything will always be in balance.

In looking at these patterns, it has often times been taught that another is to blame. There truly is no blame. Remember that you attract back the same vibration that you put out into the universe. When you send out a vibration that is attached to your emotion, not everyone will choose to respond to your vibration, you see. That is a choice. Know that you will be attracting the vibration of a person or situation and it will be in perfect balance to the same vibration that you sent, with the same intensity. The Earth is filled with people sending and receiving vibrations through their emotions every day, attracting back the same vibrations. The universe has the job of matching them up. Each of you is accountable for your own choices. There is no blame.

When your intentions have low vibrating emotions attached to them such as anger, contempt, frustration, and indifference, you are creating and attracting something less than positive, something that surely will not feel good when it returns to you. When your intent and the attached emotions have a positive focus such as love, gratitude, honor, and respect, as you release those vibrations, you are creating and attracting something positive, you see, something that will feel good to you when it returns. The key is in the emotion attached to the intention and the thought.

Here is an easy exercise that you can practice to experience the outcome. Do not forget to have fun with your experimentation and exercises. Begin with something small and simple, where you can easily and quickly experience and enjoy the outcome. Once you have successfully tried something small, move on to something bigger that may take more time to receive the outcome so that you can notice the path and to learn and to understand the patterns and the twists and turns.

You can start with an attraction of a smile. Set your intention that you are receiving smiles everywhere you go. State an affirmation to start your day, "I am receiving and enjoying smiles from others, every day, everywhere I go." Trust it, believe it and experience the emotions of receiving a smile. Smiles feel loving, gentle, caring, and supportive. In other words, *live it* in the sense that you are already experiencing those emotions from receiving the smiles.

If you think that not everyone is smiling at you, let go of that thought or intention (along with the attached emotion); that is your mental mind interfering. Stay focused on your intentions, *go to the light* and experience that you are receiving smiles and <u>only</u> that intention and those wonderful emotions. Let go of emotions that may carry vibrations of blame, excuses, or frustration. You only wish to attract the opportunity, to experience, and to witness the pattern and to receive and enjoy the result of love and success. Do not stray from that intention, your belief, and the emotions attached to it. Continue to attach the emotions that you experience from a warm smile. Feel it and expect it, and experience the joy of it. Live it. *Notice what happens.*

It is easy to get caught up in the appearance that the experiment is not working. It takes your *will* to re-set any stray emotions that might take you off track. Stay on track, *go to the light*, and remain focused on your intention and focused on experiencing and receiving only positive emotions. You wish to attract only the highest vibrations.

You can create and attract compliments. Does it feel good to receive a compliment? Does it feel good to give a compliment? Set your intention with positive emotions in place and believe that you are receiving fun and loving compliments. Start with using an intention such as, "I am receiving fun and loving compliments, from everyone, at all times." Continue to speak and trust in this intention and feel how good it is to experience that emotion. Believe in the intention and attach an emotion with a high vibration, such as joy, love, and gratitude. Stay focused and go *to the light.*

Experience that emotion in your heart, just as you do when you receive any wonderful compliment. Live that emotion. Feel the joy and the satisfaction and the comfort of receiving compliments. Stay focused on your intention and the experience of the emotion and do not stray. Live it and breathe it. Watch your creation and notice the patterns. *Notice what happens.*

You can also suggest or attempt to influence another person to feel sorry for you, in other words, create sympathy. It is another's choice in their response, to respond and to choose that emotion of sympathy or not. The vibrating emotion of sympathy is a low vibration. Look at the pattern. When another person chooses to feel sorry for you, you are attracting and sharing the vibration attached to that emotion. Does it feel good? Take a look at the pattern and decide if that is truly what you want.

Do you want to attract the lower and heavier vibrations such as pity or sympathy or do you want to attract the high vibrations of love, respect, assistance, information, and honor that are very light and feel good and pure? You can choose love, assistance and information which are high vibrations or you can choose to attract the opposite vibrations of *feeling sorry* for yourself and attracting the same from others. The emotion of sympathy would feel heavy and weigh you down while the emotions of love, information, and assistance can feel very light and uplifting. Which would you rather feel?

Do you want to attract emotions that come from your etheric (spiritual) heart such as the feeling of fulfillment or accomplishment and emotions such as respect and trust? Stating those words out loud has a vibration all its own that simply feels good. The experience in living it feels even better. You can begin any time you wish. The choice is always yours. *Go to the light* and stay focused. Be aware of what you are attracting.

Learn how energy *feels* to consciously assist in your creations. Learn how it *works* so you can understand. Another example would be to look closely at your relationship to your *worldly* or *physical* things that belong to you, and the items that you choose to keep, or the items that you choose to let go, or when you might choose to throw away your clutter. Remember, that it is all energy of course. Does the item have an emotion attached such as comfort, fear, or distrust? Maybe you received comfort or joy from an item at one time. That would be a high vibrating emotion. Notice when that emotion might change to *indifference*. Maybe you felt a *neediness* to keep an item. That would be a low vibrating emotion that you would not want to attract. Sit quietly and pay close attention to the emotion that you notice with an item or a belonging. Does it feel good or joyful? Does it weigh you down or bring fear? Does is feel *yucky*? Does it feel light and uplifting?

Be aware of your emotion attached to the thought or act of giving an item away or selling an item. Notice the emotions that are attached to the releasing of the item. Be aware of the emotion attached to the *thing(s)* that you have chosen to hold onto for so long. Is a there a high or low vibrating emotion attached to it? Are you going through the act of releasing these objects with love in your heart, or with frustration, fear, or doubt?

This could be an interesting experiment to learn more about your attachment to your physical belongings and discover what emotions you may have attached to these items. This can assist in better understanding energy and also in choosing what belongings you may want to keep or what you may want to release, depending on the emotion that is attached. Does the emotion feel good or does it feel the opposite? Remember to give gratitude and thanks as you throw away or release those items that you have decided you no longer need and know that have already served a purpose for you.

As you release these items, attach very beautiful and very high vibrating emotions to your thoughts and actions. Experience the emotions of love, gratitude, and excitement for the new space that you are now making, allowing for new high vibrating emotions to come into your life. Know that the items you are releasing are now going to serve a new purpose for someone or something else, even if they are going to re-purpose the soil. Stay focused and *go to the light*.

When you stop believing in what you can create, you stop believing in yourself. When you do not believe in yourself, you create a vibration and a reflection for others to not believe in you as well, as the universe is always balanced. It is important to always begin with yourself, as you create this reflection, as you are creation. You create a giant ripple effect in your beliefs and in your attached emotions. It is a matter of noticing and understanding the patterns and choosing to create what you desire. You are the creator and you can create anything that you desire. You must start however by believing and trusting in yourself.

Keep in mind that you cannot change others, as they too have free will, the same as you. However, you can be an example and provide loving vibrations that assist and support others. That is the ripple effect. So by experiencing and attracting high vibrating emotions, you can not only bring joy to yourself, you can also share those vibrations of joy out into the universe for others to receive and experience. When you choose to share vibrations that are the opposite, of a low vibration, remember, that is also what you are sharing with others. You are one, and you are all interconnected in your experiences and growth. The greater you raise your vibrations, the greater and more positive the impact you will have on others. This impact is greater than you can ever imagine.

When you stop believing in yourself and your ability to create, you stop believing that you can learn; the learning, creating, and growing then stop within you. You will then be filling yourself with the emotions attached to that lack of belief. These could be emotions of defeat, failure, depression, or sadness. You will then be attracting from those emotions. You will likely be attracting what you do not want to create. The choice is always yours.

Every person, every action, and every situation is energy, with emotions attached to that energy. There are many possibilities for lessons, as well as many possibilities for growth and enjoyment, as everything is energy. Opportunities for lessons, growth, and enjoyment never stop, just as creation never stops. You can choose to step into the flow and *go to the light* and feel the joy, or you can choose to be out of the flow and feel the opposite. The choice is always yours. It is your free will.

So when you *go to the light*, you follow your desires to create and experience high vibrating emotions that feel wonderful. Your Divine Source, the Angels, and your guides will continue to assist you in that direction to *go to the light* and in being *in the flow*. You may also, of course, make a choice to not follow the guidance, and then you are on your own, so to speak. You are steering against that flow and you will experience your lessons with more difficulty and with vibrations and emotions that are not of love and enjoyment, that are heavy and do not feel good. Following your guidance allows you to better breeze through your lessons with more enjoyment, love, and more ease in life.

There will always be movement, lessons, and growth. You will always have options to choose the path. Which path do you choose?

Chapter Five
Ask Your Angels

Chapter Five: Ask Your Angels

This chapter is dedicated to *asking*. You are being asked to trust in your Divine Source, the Angels, and your guides and to ask for assistance. The guidance has always been there, whether you asked or not. This chapter is serves as a reminder of sorts, to bring to your attention to ask your Angels and know and trust that they are there.

Ask yourself, "Am I ready to <u>hear</u> the answer? Do I really want to know? Am I ready to listen and take action based upon that answer, information, or the guidance? Am I ready to be *in the flow*?

The Angels and your guides come from a realm that sees and knows far more than you can possibly see, know, or remember in your physical body. They are perfect for guiding you to *go to the light*. So you might ask the questions such as, "Just what can I ask an Angel? How often can I ask?" You might think or say, "I don't want to bother them with too many questions or too many requests, as they are so busy."

Let's just say, you can ask an Angel for any assistance any time and you can ask an Angel any question. There are no time lines or schedules in that realm. Everything is in the present in the non-physical and there are no restrictions in time and space. In other words, anything is possible. Be aware there are some questions where the answer may be, that *that information will not be given to you at this time*, as it may not be time for you to have that information, know that all questions are answered, even if the answer is not ready to be shared.

Do you often catch yourself talking to yourself or talking out loud when no one else is around? You are most definitely being heard. The trick is to not only to recognize that your Angels and your guides are there listening, <u>always</u>, but to recognize that that they are there for <u>you</u>. Be aware that they can only step in to assist you if they are welcomed or invited by you. This is the law of *free will*. You and only you have the *free will* to make your choices.

You are the one who benefits and the one who experiences the results of following your choices, whether that benefit or result is one that feels good to you or not. If the result of your choice does not feel good, again, you are the one that has the *free will* to make another choice and create a different outcome. Remember to invite your Angels and trust. Invite them often, with a very loving emotion attached, of course.

When you ask an Angel for assistance, know and trust that they are by your side before you can finish your request. Also know that they will always respond. Note that the response may be a *blank* some of the time when that information is not going to be given yet as it may not be time for you to know that answer. The response might look differently then what you were imagining in your mental mind, so remember to be *open* and flexible as to how you receive the information, and trust that it will be perfect for you. Always attach a high vibrating emotion, of course.

Have you ever experimented with making choices? As it has been presented, everything is energy, so experimenting with choices would be experimenting with energy. So you are being challenged again to experiment with the energy of your choices, and you are invited to experiment again, specifically with the <u>vibration of the emotion attached to your intention</u> in those choices.

As previously discussed, when you send out a vibration into the universe, expect to receive the same vibration in return. There is no other way. All must be in balance at all times. You may not recognize this vibration as your own, but know that it is so. If you choose to intend the emotion of *hate*, expect to attract a matching vibration such as anger, for example. If you choose to intend the emotion of *love*, expect to attract a matching vibration such as *joy*.

What you attract can come from <u>anyone</u> or <u>anything</u>. It may not come from the same origin where the intention began. So, if the intent of the emotion of *hate* is for a specific object, let's say a piano or a specific person you know, do not expect that the matching vibration attracted to be surrounding that piano or that person. You can attract the creation from any other person or any other situation or object. Like vibrations attract. It is possible to come from the same source, but it does not have to. You attract in the universe, and the universe is very big.

In focusing on the emotion, you can choose that emotion with greater awareness, using one, of course, with a high vibration, in order to create or attract the benefit or result that you want, of that higher vibration. This would be the time to *ask your Angels* for assistance. They can assist in reminding you to remain focused on high vibrating emotions as well as on providing thoughts and ideas for high vibrating emotions.

It is recommended that you document your experiments with the outcomes. You can use a journal and be simple with your documentation. You do not have to write a book. You will want to begin by writing down what you wish to create (your intention or an affirmation) and choosing the emotion and the result that you wish to experience and attract. It is recommended that you always choose a high vibrating emotion with your intention, one that feels perfect to you. Do you wish to feel joy, love, and peace of mind or calm? Do you enjoy a fun vibration such as curiosity or laughter? You get to choose. Choose wisely as this is what you are will be creating and attracting. By all means, look within your heart for what *feels* wonderful to you.

You can begin with your focus, an affirmation of intent, such as, "I wish to laugh." Adjust that focus to be a <u>present</u> experience, such as "I am experiencing and attracting laughter and fun." Attach the emotion you feel with this experience. What emotion do you feel when you are laughing and having fun? The emotion can be lightheartedness, joy deep inside, or one of pure pleasure. Feel that emotion when you are putting that intention out there. That is a vibration that will attract a like vibration. And remember, if you need a little assistance in the perfect intention or emotion, *ask your Angels*.

You live in a physical world and in a physical body. It can be very powerful to put that intention out there in a physical way, by writing down your intention. Affirmations can be written such as, "I am experiencing laughter and fun with every person. I am enjoying myself and I am laughing." Read, think, and believe and experience the emotion of those affirmations over and over again. Experience the fun, excitement, pleasure, and the joy.

Know that when you begin your intention or affirmation with the words, *I am*, this is very powerful. You are giving instructions to the universe. The universe receives those instructions and the vibrations of the emotions immediately, and the vibrations begin to shift, to bring to you in return that exact same vibration, bringing all into balance. This is the most powerful way you can begin an intention or affirmation, so be very sure that vibration and emotion which you are putting out there when you begin an *"I am"* thought or statement, is the vibration that you truly want to attract and receive.

You want to be mindful to choose a vibration and intention that is positive and uplifting, not the opposite. You do not want to intend, for example, an affirmation with an emotion that you do not want to attract. When you do so, guess what, you have just used the words and emotions of what you do not want to receive, so expect to be attracting just that.

When you might think for example that you do _not_ want to hit that car, focusing on that thought and the emotion attached to _hitting that car_, attracts that vibration of the emotion. The universe accepts the vibrations from the emotions, and mirrors them right back. It does not sort it out by what you meant; it sorts it out by the vibration. If your emotion with that thought is fear, then watch out, as the vibration of hitting that car and that like vibration of the fear, for example, is exactly what you will be attracting. If your emotion attached to that thought is one of confidence that you will be driving and arriving safely at your destination, that is what you will receive back, a vibration matching that confidence. One is a low vibrating emotion while the other is a high vibrating emotion, attached to the same thought.

Remember that you are not alone. The Angels and your guides are there to assist. If you feel stuck, _ask your Angels_. If you appear to be allowing lower vibrations to take precedent, _ask your Angels_. If you are finding that you appear to be steering off course, _ask your Angels_.

Your Angels are just waiting to assist you, in even those requests that appear to you to be the smallest requests. They desire to assist you no matter what, to remind you or guide you to remain focused on that high vibrating emotion and vibration and attracting what it is you wish to attract. They are waiting to assist you in <u>noticing</u> when you are receiving that same high vibration back, so that you can do it again. They are waiting to assist you in <u>noticing</u> when you attract something that is not so high vibrating, that does not feel good, so you can learn and grow to attract what you wish, rather than the opposite.

So as you experiment and experience more fun and joy in your life, notice the nudges and the thoughts from the Angels that are there to assist you in continuing to attract those high vibrations. They are by your side assisting you with your growth. And remember, it is the vibration attached to the emotion that attracts. So you decide what it will be.

If you appear to be off track in what you wish to attract, *ask your Angels* for the guidance to assist you in getting back on track to fulfill your wishes and your creations. The Angels are there supporting you at all times, whether you are attracting what you desire or the opposite. It only makes sense to *ask your Angels* for assistance in attracting what feels good to you. You have your own personal specialists. That is their job, and trust that the Angels <u>love</u> their jobs.

They are delighted to be working and have few boundaries in their jobs, other than acknowledging your free will.

Remember that there are Angels on each and every one of the "Rays of Light." Remember that each of those rays is of a different frequency and a different color. Each of the Angels assists in bringing in a specific frequency, the frequency of that ray, the one that is perfect for what you need at that time. Those frequencies of the "Rays of Light," and the Angels assigned to that ray or that frequency, are there to assist with a specific vibration that you are emitting and attracting. So let's say you have been struggling with *hate* or with *depression*. The Angels and the "Rays of Light" bringing in all of the frequencies will have the perfect frequency and the perfect Angels to assist you with that particular vibration. But remember, you must ask and allow the Angels to step in and assist you. You <u>must</u> be open and know that you so deserve that love and assistance.

When you *ask your Angels*, you need not be concerned with which Angel to ask; trust that you will receive the assistance and the guidance from the perfect Angel for your situation or request. The Angels and the "Rays of Light" will sort that out for you. By asking, you will receive assistance. It's that easy. By allowing, you have opened the door for assistance beyond your understanding and comprehension. By accepting your Angels assistance, you have accepted these frequencies. These frequencies provide what you need at that exact time for that exact given situation, and what is perfect for you.

Yes, there are many Angels and Archangels that you may have familiarity with, such as Archangel Michael or Archangel Gabrielle. They each have frequencies and can offer assistance for the vibration presenting itself. Each specific frequency is for the purpose of assisting with a specific vibration. It is not necessary for you to know and understand each Angel and their frequency. It is only important to understand how it works. By all means if you feel guided to ask a specific Angel or you enjoy asking a particular Archangel, please do so. They may be guiding you to ask them as they are carrying the exact frequencies you need at that time. Do not hesitate to follow the guidance.

Also remember that there are an infinite number of rays with an infinite number of frequencies and, of course, an infinite number of Angels. When you *ask your Angels*, the correct Angel and frequency steps in based on the vibration you have put out there to work with you and support you, no matter what vibration you are putting out there. There are no exceptions; everyone in a physical body can ask an Angel for assistance. And I do mean <u>everyone</u>.

In this physical world it is also difficult to comprehend that Angels can assist an infinite number of you at any given time. In the realm of the Angels, there is no time and space and all is infinite. It is very different than time as you know it on this planet. Many of you have asked or wondered, "How this is possible? Can an Angel really be everywhere and with everyone at the same time?" Yes, not only is this possible, but it happens every day. Don't ever put out a vibration of <u>concern</u> or worry over these questions and remember to trust and believe that not only is it possible, it is occurring every moment of every day. Take those low vibrations off of your shoulders and put them right onto the laps and the shoulders of the Angels by asking for assistance. They will take care of it. *Next, watch to see how it's done.*

So let's get back to your experiment. When you are experimenting and you *ask your Angels*, just trust and know that you will be receiving and deserving of the perfect Angel to assist you with your vibrations. Then you must learn to listen for the guidance and truly *hear* the guidance, or learn how to *listen to the dark* as will be discussed in the next chapter, Chapter 6.

You must learn to understand and follow the guidance for the best possible outcome. Be flexible and learn to take chances as you follow that little voice, that thought, or that vision in your head. The Angels will teach you as you go. Pay close attention to your lessons. When you follow the guidance and that little thought or idea, watch where it leads you. See where it takes you, and notice the outcome. Then do it all over again. Have fun with it. The Angels love to have fun. It gets easier and easier the more you practice.

That is what this is about, practice. Don't be surprised at the fun and spontaneity this can bring into your life. Set your expectations and your emotions for the positive result and let the Angels direct you. The Angels can see through the fog. The Angels can guide you in the dark, and assist you in your steering through the fog. Angels can assist you in steering when you cannot see what's ahead of you, when you are in the dark. That is their purpose and they love what they do. The Angels <u>LOVE</u> their jobs.

In you are working on lower vibrations, such as *anger* or *hate*, do not be concerned. The Angels assist with all vibrations. They can assist you in letting go of the vibrations that do not feel good to you and teach you to attract the vibrations that do feel good. They are asking you to step on board the boat and set your course full steam ahead. They are just waiting for you to ask. No matter what the vibration, there are Angels to assist.

The "Rays of Light" are here for everyone. They are frequencies to balance the light and the dark and to balance and assist with all the vibrations, high and low. They are here to assist you in cleansing and balancing your physical body. They are here teach you and assist you in understanding *how it works*. And they are here to bring to you the Angels and the guidance. The angels are alive with joy, working within each ray and within that specific frequency to assist you with your vibrations. You need only ask.

As you continue to experiment, be sure to watch for the patterns. Learn the patterns of the vibrations and attraction. As you watch, you will soon understand how it works and will be creating vibrations that feel better and better. You will learn which vibrations feel good and which do not, and you will learn how to create that which feels good and how to obtain the resulting emotion that you desire, with the perfect outcome.

Take one step at a time, one or two Angels at a time, whatever you wish or desire. Each step may appear to be little, but when you look back, you will truly see how big your steps have been. They quickly turn into giant steps and your vibrations have suddenly changed to attract more of what feels good and is perfect for you, rather than the opposite. Look at you and what you are creating! You have suddenly moved far beyond what you imagined. You can go as far as you like, as the universe is vast and infinite, and let it be known, you are working with the Divine, the universe, and "all that is."

Chapter Six
Listen To the Dark

Chapter Six: Listen to the Dark

Listen to the dark, for darkness speaks. Darkness is truth, wisdom and opportunity. You come into this world into darkness, without remembrance. Light is truth, wisdom, and remembrance. Dark turns into light, and light turns into dark, in a circular pattern, creating a balance. As a human being, you were born into this darkness. Humans have been walking and living in darkness for thousands of years, searching for remembrance through the light. It is this pattern of light and dark that allows growth.

What is interesting is that you were not born with enough remembrance, to fully know what you are missing. You appear to be searching for that magic key, the one that will unlock the door to the light, but you do not have enough information and remembrance to know where to go or where to begin. Many of you appear to be finding keys, and many may very well be finding keys. However, in being human, there is the appearance of many humans going in many different directions, some out of the flow and some in the flow. Some of you are following true guidance and some of you are following your mental mind, not understanding the difference between your mental mind and your etheric (spiritual) heart.

The key to the light is very simple, far easier then you could imagine. The key to light and remembrance is found in listening to the dark. You have been given symbols, clues, guidance, and all your senses in this physical world to assist you. As truth is both light and dark, it will elevate you, support growth, and systematically allow more light, balance, and remembrance. You need only to *listen to the dark*.

The ultimate goal is to balance the light and dark. This is accomplished with truth, wisdom, and the opportunity of your growth in the dark, allowing the remembrance from the light. But how do you recognize the difference after living in darkness for so many years? You must trust your feelings as they are real. You must trust your voices, as they are real. Most importantly, you must trust yourselves and the Divine guidance. You must trust and believe. This is not an easy task, as much of your lives you have been taught the opposite, out of tradition and patterns. That is what was believed to be truth. This type of truth lies in your human mental mind. The real truth lies in your etheric (spiritual) heart, where you are all connected, as one. The real truth comes from you and your communication with the Divine as you bring in the light and remember "all that is." The real truth is your truth.

Let's begin with darkness and the lack of light under which you were born as human. Your etheric soul enters your human body, into the darkness, leaving behind your remembrance, your truth, and remembrance of "all that is." The light and remembrance represents the truth about your soul, before entering the human body. Your soul's human life truly begins at the time your soul enters your physical body, not at the time of conception. Upon conception, the physical body begins to physically develop in the womb. On the third day after your conception, your soul enters your human body. This is the true beginning of human life. At that time, there is darkness, truth, wisdom, and lack of remembrance.

When your soul leaves your human body, remembrance returns to the soul. This is when your body loses its life as you know it in your human form. Your soul continues to live. Your remembrance may occur in stages and is determined by each soul. One soul might choose to stay within the earthly plane at that level of remembrance, while another soul may choose to step into the light of full remembrance, with truth and wisdom. This is due to your free will, which is always guaranteed, so to speak, to each human being and to each of you as souls. You are all blessed with your free will at all times.

What is it like living in the dark? You can all share in the answer to that question. More importantly, better questions to address would be, "What is it like living in the light?" or "How do you find the light, and remembrance?" Hence the answer lies in the title of this chapter, "Listen to the Dark." This now brings us full circle, emphasizing the importance of the balance between the dark and light.

There is a delicate and subtle balance between dark and light. You must truly listen to the dark for your directions, guidance, and bringing remembrance into focus. You must follow the truth from the dark, right into the light, as you grow through your opportunities. This is all accomplished through your etheric (spiritual) heart, not through the mental mind as you have been taught. The mental mind cannot fully comprehend the light as it does not have remembrance. This is why non-physical experiences are often difficult to describe. Only the etheric (spiritual) heart has the remembrance of your connection to the Divine and "all that is." In this human world you must <u>believe</u> and <u>trust</u> in what cannot always be seen or explained in a physical sense. This is a key.

It is not always easy to *listen to the dark*. This is listening to the guidance, paying attention to symbols, and to your senses. Then you put forth action, taking steps to follow the guidance or that nudge. This listening is not only the physical hearing or the knowing, but also taking action based upon the hearing and the knowing. That fleeting thought is not just a fleeting thought. It is real and it is communication. It is guidance and direction. Many of you have been ignoring this communication for years, as you believed it to not be true guidance. You may allow your mental mind to talk you out of believing, or you carry the belief that this is not following common sense. Common sense is not what you have often been taught. Common sense is actually listening to the dark and using your etheric (spiritual) heart in balance with your body, your soul, and your mental mind. Common sense is more than your mental mind alone.

Common sense comes from your willingness to explore the darkness that brings about remembrance. Truth and remembrance have always been there. It is your willingness to explore with belief and trust that unlock the door to what you are seeking. That is why your intentions are vital. Intentions are also a key. They can be a catalyst for change when you are in the dark. They can represent belief, trust, and hope. They can be hope for you in balancing the duality of both the dark and the light. Your intentions and the vibrations of your emotions that are attached to them are your steering wheel for what direction you will go and ultimately what you will create.

Divine guidance comes from many sources, all originating from your etheric (spiritual) heart. Your complete soul, in the etheric realm, has full remembrance and can assist you. This can be referred to as your higher self or your higher heart. There is also your Divine Source, the loving Angels, and your guides just waiting to assist. Angels are not allowed to assist unless you ask or invite them as they cannot interfere with your free will here in the physical world. There are guides from the etheric world also waiting at your beck and call to assist you, all you need do is to ask or invite them in. Your guides that are assisting you have previously lived in a physical body, whereas the Angels, for the most part, have not.

The physical world is very different from the etheric world, the place where guidance and direction begins. Guidance can come in the form of hearing, knowing, or seeing, for example. You can experience and receive guidance through all of your senses, feelings, and emotions. You can experience guidance through your physical bodies in seeing, touching, or smelling and you can also experience through non-physical signs, symbols, or images. You must look for the patterns in your day and recognize their meaning. You must pay attention to the symbols and the meaning in conversations, on billboards, in a poster, on a license plate, or in a phone number. The blindness, or darkness, allows a human the opportunity to learn and to grow. Understanding the darkness represents truth and wisdom and allows opportunity for growth. When you understand, embrace, and appreciate this blindness, it is a pathway.

Dark and light are neither good nor bad. It just is. It is separation and a representation, a key, path, or symbol for an opportunity to learn and to grow. The "Rays of Light" are frequencies with knowledge and remembrance and truth in the highest form. They represent "all that is" and fill in the many missing pieces of your puzzles. The "Rays of Light" represent both dark and light and make up the perfect balance. The rays are a beautiful gift available to all who are ready to choose them.

The wisdom lies in the dark, not in logic or whatever your mental mind might suggest. This darkness offers the opportunity for you to follow your etheric (spiritual) heart and Divine guidance. Look for the patterns. Create an understanding of the patterns. Remember, they are neither good nor bad, just patterns. Patterns in the dark and the light continue to move you forward, in growth. You must pay attention to both the light and the dark to maintain balance. Once you stop paying attention, so stops your growth and your balance.

Attraction is created by each human as you live in this physical world. It is part of your growth. Your balance is in both dark and light. Attraction occurs as part of that balance. If you carry the vibration in the emotion of worry for example, you will attract that same vibration as a balance to what you are creating. You will continue that pattern until you learn the pattern and understand how you are creating that pattern. That attraction is there for as long as necessary, until that chapter or that lesson is complete and you begin another creation. Then the attraction and pattern disappears, just as quickly as it came, allowing the new attraction to step in. Watch for the patterns. What has changed and what has become complete? What is different? Look for the growth. Have you learned a lesson and have you now created an opening for a new chapter? Focus always on the positive and the growth in a positive light to attract the changes you truly wish. If your intentions and emotions are not positive, remember, you will attract just that.

Be mindful of how you react and respond in this physical world. When you are criticized by another or if someone you love chooses another, you may feel hurt or pain on an emotional level. Your mental mind may rationalize this feeling or emotion with thoughts that you have learned or been taught in the past. This blocks the truth from coming in through your emotional or etheric (spiritual) heart. You may judge or blame and create thoughts that are not positive about yourself or others.

The illusion of judgment or blame can only be found in the physical world. The vibrations will always be balanced. You attract what you are creating. It is important to focus on growth, learning, and moving forward. There is movement at all times. Do you want to be in the flow of the movement or struggling against the movement with hardship and discomfort? Which feels better? You always have choices.

If you notice that what concerned you yesterday does not concern you today, what has changed? *Listen to the dark.* How do you feel about this in your heart? Trust and believe and allow the worries to be released. If you continue to experience the emotion of worry, then you will secure that emotion tightly within you, blocking or delaying your growth. The choice is always up to you. That is your free will.

When you continue on your path with trust, staying true to your belief, you then attract that belief and all else is dissolved. Yesterday's emotion of concern is no longer a concern; it has dissolved and you have now attracted your belief, your high vibrating emotion. It is truly that simple. This is a law of the universe. You attract what you believe and experience, in your heart and in your soul, for they each speak very loudly to the universe and the universe responds with great consistency and accuracy.

If you choose to stop believing, your affirmation and goal has been re-routed to one of distrust and the emotion attached to that distrust, such as fear or jealousy. Expect to attract just that, as that changes your belief and your intention. Expect, now to attract something very different than what you had originally desired. This is a law of the universe.

There is a tendency to look for confirmation as you are creating. That is being human and is neither good nor bad; it is just part of your lessons. When you ask, and you believe and trust, you will receive confirmation in surprising ways. You just need to pay attention and recognize that confirmation when it shows. Stay true to your intentions and affirmations, and your emotions, or you will change your course and the outcome. No matter how murky or turbulent the waters appear, remember this is illusion. Stay true in the dark, listening, to bring in the wisdom, growth, light, remembrance, and ultimately, balance, with your original desired outcome.

True guidance from the Divine Source comes from your etheric (spiritual) heart. Guidance designed to assist you with staying organized in the physical world comes from your mental mind. Your mental mind does not understand the non-physical world, while your etheric (spiritual) heart does. When you use your mental mind for emotional guidance, rather than using your etheric heart, this is not true guidance and it becomes confusing and can even be chaotic. Mental guidance is coming from the physical world, your old mental memories, lessons, and patterns. While your mental mind is perfect for assisting you with the patterns needed for living and surviving and being organized in a physical world, it is not designed to replace true guidance from your etheric (spiritual) heart.

Your mental mind develops from what you learn in this physical world. This is what is commonly referred to as common sense, coming from your experience in the physical world, or from what you have been taught. As you are growing up, you learn numbers, memorize spelling of words and definitions, and are taught other's thoughts and ideas. But remember, true common sense is a balance of your mind, your body, and your soul, coming from both your etheric (spiritual) heart and your mental mind.

Your mental mind is necessary for you to live and survive in a physical world. This is also where your ego lies. The mental mind keeps you on track for organization in the physical world; however, it takes you off track when used for emotional guidance that is meant to come from your etheric (spiritual) heart. When you attempt to use your mental mind for emotional guidance, you lose focus on what is real as you begin to rationalize your thought and talk yourself out of truth. Thoughts such as, "No, this couldn't be it. There's no way this would work. No, I want something different. I don't want to turn that direction." Your mental mind can confuse you, side track you, take you on a detour, block you, trick you, and most of all, tell you that it's not true, when that actually is the truth.

Your emotional mind comes directly from your Divine Source, through your etheric (spiritual) heart. This is pure truth and remembrance that is not learned in the physical world. What comes from our emotional heart is not learned by memorizing numbers, ideas, and formulas; it just is. There is a difference between the physical world and the non-physical, etheric world. It is a matter of understanding *how it works*.

When you receive information from your mental mind, you might be thinking it over and referencing information that you learned in school, on the job, or from your experience in general. You would be thinking it over in your mind, looking at options, and determining what makes sense according to what you have learned in the physical world.

An example would be when conducting an investigation about a situation; you would gather all of the physical facts that you have and line the pros and cons on the table for review. You might then look for patterns and consistencies, as well as inconsistencies, based upon your experience in the physical world. You would access all that you have learned in a physical sense to draw conclusions based on those facts. Yet, you may be missing some of the information if you are not accessing your intuition, your gut, or that little voice in your head, your etheric (spiritual) heart. How many times have there been mistakes in a court of law when a person is being tried based on only the known facts? Yet, you may not have all of the facts.

When receiving information from your emotional mind, from your Divine Source, it is very different. Often this difference is subtle. In fact, it can be so subtle, that you often miss the guidance. You may find it a challenge to recognize it or to understand the difference. As an example, again in conducting an investigation, you might receive direct guidance or information from your etheric (spiritual) heart that may be difficult to explain.

A person may not yet have all the facts, but may receive information from the heart that says, "This is what happened." You may not have all of the physical facts at that

moment in time; however, what you have learned to call
your gut feeling, which is your etheric (spiritual) guidance,
has provided a knowing that is often hard to explain. This
knowing is actually guidance from your etheric (spiritual)
heart and your Divine Source. This knowing could provide
enough information to assist you in gathering more facts
that are necessary for a court, and a clear conclusion. This
would be using your mental mind, body, and your soul for
common sense in gathering all of the facts.

It is important not to confuse the guidance or information
from your etheric (spiritual) heart with your mental mind
stepping in to provide the logical answer that you may
prefer or may expect. This is that subtle difference. It is only
when you understand them both that you will recognize the
difference. That recognition comes only from experience
and practice.

Here are more simple examples to assist you in
understanding information coming from your etheric
(spiritual) heart. How many of you experienced thinking
about a person, the phone rings, and there is that person
calling you. Or, maybe you run into that person the next day.
How many of you can finish a sentence or a word for a
person that is speaking and just *know* it, although you are
not sure why you just *know* it? That is no accident. Have you
ever had words come out of your mouth and wondered
where they came from as you certainly did not think about
saying those words? Have you ever walked into a new

environment, somewhere you have never been, yet everything looks and feels familiar to you? You are connecting with your etheric (spiritual) heart and another realm of information, yet you may not be aware of it.

Explanations have been used from the reference of your physical world, as you were wearing blinders, to explain away these occurrences. There is a tendency out of habits and old patterns to seek a logical explanation, referenced in your physical world, rather than to look at the truth, as it may feel a bit scary. The more you understand the more your fears will dissipate.

You know when you have had experiences that you are not able to explain. It is common, and you have been taught to find an explanation in your mental mind, that comes from a physical world. Not all explanations and answers truly come from your physical world, but that is what you have been taught most of the time. That is the reason for this book, to better know and understand the answers and information that come from the mental mind, in the physical world, and to better know and understand the information and answers and information that come from your emotional or etheric (spiritual) heart, in the non-physical realm.

Watch for the signs to affirm and to guide you. Notice them, write and them down to remember the patterns so that you can recognize and understand them for the purpose of learning.

You live in a physical body in and a physical world. The two worlds of physical and the non-physical must be balanced. The two worlds are both necessary. This is not something to be judged but <u>to be understood.</u> This is not to be learned as much as it is to be understood. You do not have to physically work hard; you must put forth action toward your growth, to experience, practice, and to understand. Take action steps such as practicing with a different approach, paying attention to your emotions, meditating, listening for guidance, or using positive affirmations. Remember, it is the vibrations in your emotions of judgment and blame that can stop you from learning. It is your fear and your ego telling you something different that can block you from remembrance and experiencing truth, love, and the bliss of the non-physical. You create in this physical world exactly what you want to believe.

Recognize that you cannot truly change another or choose for others. You may attempt to advise and direct another; however, they too have free will. If they choose to bend to meet your expectations, look at the pattern that you are creating for both of you. Maybe they are learning to do as you say rather than listening to their own Angels and the guidance. Is that truly what you want? If you find yourself with the intentions to *change* another, be mindful that is pattern of interfering with or controlling others that can block their growth as well as your own. Notice the low vibrating emotions attached to those intentions. This may create the exact <u>opposite</u> of what you desire.

It is important to be very mindful in setting your intentions, so that your intention is exactly what you do want to attract. You may learn that the job you just acquired through setting your intentions may not be what you truly desire after all. In retrospect, you decided you wanted <u>that job</u>, and only <u>that job</u>. A better intention might be to acquire the job that is perfect for you and leave it to the universe to attract that perfect job. There may be another job out there that would bring you far more happiness. The universe holds an infinite number of options whereas as a human, you are vastly more limited in knowing your options. A better option might be to intend high vibrating emotions for what is perfect for you.

Below are some guidelines to assist you in *listening to the dark*:

<u>Actions to Embrace For Creating and Attracting Growth in the Dark</u>

1. Use, think, and imagine words and thoughts that carry high vibrating emotions, such as the emotions of love, joy, bliss, gratitude, and peace. Think and speak in a positive and uplifting manner rather than the opposite.
2. Practice loving and kind acts towards others, remembering to do the same with yourself.

3. Understand and practice using discernment. The definition of discernment is often misunderstood. Discernment is more than recognizing judgment and blame and seeing and understanding the difference. True discernment goes a step further in truly practicing and *letting go* of the judgment and blame. It would mean viewing situations, others' actions and other human beings without <u>experiencing</u> the emotions such as judgment and blame and reacting accordingly. This would also mean adopting a more uplifting view in choosing high vibrating emotions such as curiosity, love, and understanding, and <u>living it</u>, as you experience situations.

4. Ask your Divine Source, the Angels, and your guides for guidance and assistance.

5. Access and allow the frequencies of the "Rays of Light" to shine through you. You need only use your intentions. Ask and you shall receive so to speak. You can use the meditations in Chapter 8, the healing sessions in Chapters 11 and 12, or the <u>Prayer of Love and Protection</u> found in Chapters 8, 11, 12 and in the Conclusion.

6. Use meditations, whether they are simple and brief, or set aside more *quiet* time for you to assist you in letting go of low vibrating emotions. Meditations are described and discussed in more detail in Chapter 7. You will find specific formal meditations to use in Chapter 8.

Here is a brief guide to understanding the difference between your communication from your etheric (spiritual) heart (clear communication from the Angels and your guides), and your communication from your mental mind (your streaming thoughts and *self-talk* that seem to never shut off).

This is likely listening to your mental mind:

1. Is it your voice in your head arguing with your thoughts?
2. Are your thoughts harmful to other persons in any way?
3. Are you talking yourself out of a thought or idea, one that is not harmful?
4. Does the information or answer bring you down or make you feel heavy and weighted?
5. Are you asking questions or seeking information while you are experiencing strong emotions such as confusion, anger, fear, anxiousness, confusion, etc.?
6. Are you repeating thoughts or worries and obsessing over them in your head?
7. Are you *receiving* thoughts or information, or possibly guidance, and you decide in your head you do not agree.
8. Are you confused and in an agitated state grasping for a quick answer out of a current emotion you are experiencing?

This is likely listening to your etheric (spiritual) heart:

1. Does the answer or information come before you finish asking the thought or question?
2. Does it feel good or perfect when you receive the information?
3. Does the information or answer feel uplifting and light rather than the opposite?
4. When you receive a thought or idea or look at an object and say to yourself, "That's it!" or "That is perfect." and know that it is true.
5. Did the thought or idea appear to pop into your head out of nowhere?
6. Did you walk into a shop and immediately walk directly up to a piece of clothing or an object that was exactly what you wanted?
7. Are you asking questions or receiving information and guidance while you are experiencing emotions that are peaceful and relaxing or when you are in a meditative state?
8. Are you experiencing or receiving everything you are intending or wanting as if it were magically materializing in front of your eyes? You are likely attracting these outcomes by attaching high vibrating emotions to your intentions or affirmations.
9. Are the words coming out of your mouth and they are words that you are not thinking in your head?
10. Do you *just know* and do not know why you *just know*?

11. Are you receiving thoughts, suggestions, or ideas and you do not know where they are coming from? Do these thoughts feel good and uplifting and are not harmful to anyone?

Keys to Assist in *Listening to the Dark*:

1. Balance your mental mind with your body and soul in all aspects, recognize and understand your mental mind and its purpose, as well as your etheric (spiritual) heart and its purpose.
2. Balance and care for your body's nourishment with your food and drink. Addictions or too much of any one thing going into your body can create an imbalance, interfering with your ability to clearly *listen in the dark*. You must listen to your body to recognize what feels balanced to you. When feeling *out of sorts*, pay attention to what your body may need or what may have been excessive to cause this feeling or experience and create an imbalance. It may be helpful to remove certain foods or drinks from your diet and re-introduce them in a more balanced way, paying close attention to how you respond. Take notes and look for patterns.
3. Care for your physical body itself. Providing physical and healthy movement to your body on a consistent basis allows the energy to flow and interact between the physical and the non-physical. The movement

also keeps your physical body from becoming stagnant and deteriorating from lack of use. Your bodies were meant to be used and cared for with the emotion of love.

4. Quiet your mind to allow yourself to listen. Quiet your mind to open your etheric (spiritual) heart and allow the light to enter. It is difficult to hear in the dark when you surround yourself with distractions, such as constant T.V. or loud music. Remove yourself from distractions and replace it with the sounds of nature, peaceful meditation, quiet time, and comforting, soft music. Bathe in sea salt, Epsom salts or essential oils to soothe and sort your thoughts. Take time out for some gentle exercise. Let go of your mental thoughts and emotions that feel heavy and do not feel uplifting. Experiment to determine what feels perfect to you. Don't be afraid to choose something different. Remember to treat and reward yourself with this often. It is important and you deserve it. Use the meditations referenced in Chapters 7 and 8.

5. Understand the difference between your mental mind and etheric (spiritual) heart and learn to balance both the physical and the non-physical in a physical world. The mental mind is to keep you organized in a physical world, allowing you to build things, balance your check book, add numbers, take care of your physical body, and in organizing your physical belongings. This is necessary.

Your etheric (spiritual) heart is to assist in your connection to your true guidance, your Divine Source and "all that is." Nurture your soul, your etheric (spiritual) heart and your emotional mind, with positive and uplifting thoughts and emotions, words, and behavior. This will attract and create what you truly desire, while you use your mental mind to stay organized in this physical world. Learn to use your etheric (spiritual) heart for the guidance and to attract high vibrations such as love.

6. Understand *how it works* so to speak, in the subtle communication you are receiving. You may very well need to unlearn and change the past patterns and habits in order to learn and understand *how it works* in order to bring in supportive and uplifting patterns. It is important to understand the process and the patterns for listening to your Divine Source, the Angels, and your guides from the dark. For example, watch for your mental mind saying, "I don't want that. That's not where I want to go. No, that isn't what I what I want to do. That won't work." When you notice this occurring, stop, rewind, and ask yourself, "What piece of information or guidance was given to me that I chose to ignore or that I decided I did not want to follow?"

7. Be open and believe and trust in what you are sensing, hearing, knowing, seeing, and feeling.

8. Always focus on what is positive and uplifting rather than the opposite to assist in your *listening to the dark.*

At first, it may be common to argue with the communication that is given to you by your Divine Source, the Angels, and your guides, as this is often what you've been taught in the past from past patterns and old habits. You may want to discount the information, to over analyze it, or to ignore that communication. Pay close attention to the guidance which can come to you in many forms. Pay special attention if the answer or response comes before you have finished asking the question or having the thought, for this is true guidance. The more you practice the more you will understand. The more you understand the easier it will become. This can become your new habit and your new pattern.

Chapter Seven
What is Meditation?

Chapter Seven: What is Meditation?

Just what is meditation? How many of you have asked that question? It will continue to be asked and the answers will always be different. Meditation is unique to each of you. Meditation is personal and the perfect meditation for you may not be the perfect meditation for another. It is whatever works and feels right for you. That is why the answer will always be different.

The purpose of this chapter is to create an awareness of meditation and a start for you to determine what meditation means to you. The information may feel a little vague, however, that is due to the practice of meditation being very unique for every individual, including the definition of what it means. Once you have awareness, you can read examples in chapters to follow and gain more incite as to the different types of meditations that are being used. You will then be creating what it means to you.

Meditation allows you to connect to your Divine Source, the Angels, or your guide, in whatever manner feels right to you. Whatever your belief may be, meditation aids you in connecting with that belief and with the non-physical to receive and experience the benefits of that connection.

The meditations in the next chapter of this book are a starting point. They are to assist you in seeing what meditation might look like or to experience what a meditation might feel like for you. The meditations in

Chapter 8 are formal meditations that connect you more deeply with another realm. In order to connect more deeply and to receive the greatest benefit, it is recommended that these five steps be included in your meditation.

Below is a guideline, listing the five recommended steps to be used in meditation:

(1) Protect yourself in the physical and non-physical. You can use the "Prayer of Love and Protection" that is used in the meditations in Chapter 8, in the healing sessions in Chapters 11 and 12, and provided in the Conclusion. This protection allows only the highest vibrations to be received while you are in a state of receiving.

(2) Ask for assistance from your Divine Source, the Angels, your guide, the beings of the "Rays of Light, "or from your personal belief in a Divine being.

(3) Ask to receive the frequencies of the "Rays of Light," the Earth energies, and the vibration of love through your intentions and desires, and be open to receiving, knowing that you are deserving.

(4) Choose high vibrating emotions to attract the greatest outcome.

(5) Give gratitude and appreciation for the assistance.

When you ask for assistance in a meditation or in a "Rays of Light" session, you can substitute in accordance with your belief. When choosing to meditate for example, when you ask for the assistance from an Angel, your guide, or a Divine being, you can always substitute in accordance to your beliefs, as long as your belief can be considered coming from the love of the Divine. It must be of *unconditional love*. In the "Rays of Light" sessions (Chapters 11 and 12), it is recommended that you ask for assistance from all of the beings of the "Rays of Light" in order to receive the greatest benefit. The choice is yours. You can certainly experiment if you wish to notice the difference.

So what works for you? That is the question. There are many types of meditations and many ways to meditate; they can be simple or more formal. You are encouraged to use meditations that feel good to you and you are encouraged to also design your own meditations, ones that are perfect for you. Why not? That is the purpose of meditation.

There are many parts of a meditation that you might have discovered that you can adjust, to what feels right or perfect for you. In other words, you are encouraged to make it work for you, as that is the point. If it does not work for you, there is no point.

Meditation can be viewed as a way to access your etheric or spiritual heart. This can also been seen as a way to *feel* better, to feel more relaxed, to access information, and to connect with the Angels or your guides, to bring calmness to yourself and into your day, to make decisions with high vibrating emotions attached to them, to be creative, to enjoy quiet time, to bring peace of mind as you let go of your mental mind, to let go of the chatter in your mental mind and bring in what feels good, and to bring in the experience of *calm*. The list can continue. Meditation can assist you with *letting go* of the low vibrating emotions that interfere with your *quiet time* and your ability to *listen to the dark* and hear the guidance.

Meditation is a process that can be defined by <u>you</u> since it is for <u>you</u>. Another's definition of meditation may not be your definition of meditation. So, you are encouraged to create, what feels good and what works for you. Using an existing meditation is very good starting point. There are many meditations that have a specific intention or purpose that may appeal to you. Use them, and remember you can also adjust them to make them your own.

When regularly and consistently using a meditation that works for you, the benefits can have no end. The benefits are beyond what a human mind can understand as they are of the *universe*. The benefits included are beyond your comprehension in this physical world, as they extend far beyond your world into the universe and beyond.

So where do you start? There are two types of formal meditations in this book, each with two variations, for the purpose of assisting you in a way that is easy and comfortable for you. These meditations can be found in Chapter 8.

Each of the meditations have a similar purpose, however, the focus of the "Guidance Meditation" is to channel the frequencies of the "Rays of Light" to assist you in clear communication and the guidance from your Divine Source, the Angels, and your guides. General healing benefits are included. The focus of the "Healing and Guidance Meditation" is to channel the frequencies of the "Rays of Light" to assist you with general healing benefits, to assist you with special intentions (including general healing intentions), to assist you with a more elevated or a deeper connection allowing greater benefits, and to assist you in clear communication and the guidance from your Divine Source, the Angels, and your guides. Both meditations can support your personal growth on all levels.

Whichever meditation is used, when accessing and asking to receive the "Rays of Light," know that it automatically comes with the assistance of the Angels on each ray, and the assistance does not stop when the session is complete. The assistance continues once you have made that connection. So, it is recommended that you continue to watch for and pay attention to the guidance. Some guidance might come right away and some guidance might come in the coming weeks or even months. There is no time limit for when you may receive the guidance.

By all means, use these meditations in a way that works best for you. Do not be afraid to adjust them, keeping in mind the recommended guideline at the start of this chapter which lists the five steps that are recommended to be included in a formal mediation. You are welcome to start from scratch if you like, creating the perfect meditation for you.

It is also suggested that you conduct research, looking at different types of meditations, and be aware of different viewpoints of others regarding meditation. You can start your research at the library. Determine which approach feels right for you. Do not be afraid to adjust a meditation for what feels perfect. This is your creation. Experiment and determine what works for you.

Some of the other types of mediations may include an individual mediation you complete alone or one that is completed in a group setting. You will find that there are many variations to meditations. There are meditations that take you as a group to a specific location (in your mind or imagination) or ones that allow you to choose the imagined location as you sit together in a group. Both can be very beneficial. Some meditations have an individual that reads the meditation to you as you close your eyes and listen, while others provide some basic direction and allow you to take the meditation where you want to go. There are many that use music that is calming and soothing or that provides frequencies and energies that are conducive to quieting your mental mind. They can all work.

A way to meditate can be as simple as setting aside *quiet time* where you are not interrupted, allowing you to simply sit quietly while letting go of any thoughts in your mental mind. It may be merely sitting in nature, listening to the sounds, absorbing, and receiving the benefits of nature's energy. It could be a walk or a run, listening to music, exercising, taking a moment to reflect, enjoying a sea salt bath or a bath with soothing oils, enjoying the scent of a flower in bloom, writing or documenting your thoughts in a diary or journal, going for a drive in the country, enjoying the sunshine on your face or skin, reflecting on beautiful memories that bring in high vibrating emotions, watching a bird or an animal in nature, or a simple affirmation that triggers high vibrating emotions.

Remember, it is always the vibrations of the emotions attached to your words and intentions that allow you to create and attract more of the same. The emotions are where the vibrations are held. If it is pleasure you want, choose the emotion that is most pleasurable to you during your meditation.

Meditations can be healthy, fun, and rewarding. Anything that brings you comfort can also be considered a form of meditation. It can be short or long, simple or more formal. If the result is bringing in a quiet and comforting emotion with a high vibration you can call it a meditation. An important key is that you must *let go* of the chatter and thoughts of your mental mind during this time.

There are some that might find it relaxing to balance their checkbook as they can do so with ease and without effort. For those this can be considered a form of mediation. Treat and reward yourself often with a simple meditation throughout the day, you deserve it. See it as a well-deserved treat. Begin to look at it a little differently as you understand what meditation might mean to you.

Another key is to practice in order to determine what works. You will clearly receive many benefits as you practice and experiment. You see there is no right or wrong; it is simply a form of reference as to what feels right.

Pay attention to what *feels* good to you and what brings you the emotions of joy. What brings you to feeling of love? Love is the highest vibrating emotion. What brings you that feeling? Incorporate whatever it is into your life, no matter how simple or how silly it might seem to you. Be sure that your meditations and intentions do no harm to another.

The formal meditations in this book can be used when you feel the guidance to do so, but do not allow a heavy emotion from an obligation to weigh you down. Start with using simple meditations throughout the day, whenever you wish. Using quick, simple ways to meditate throughout the day will allow you to associate the result of the wonderful emotion and the quickness in receiving that reward. Those simple meditations throughout the day can quickly and effectively elevate your emotions to a high vibration when you catch yourself falling into an old pattern of experiencing the opposite. Make it quick, simple, and make it is easy. You can always choose more time for your meditations or choose more formal meditations whenever you like.

Begin by noticing the simple meditations that you may already use and enjoy. Notice the new ways that you can incorporate them more often. Experiment, research, and learn, or create new ones to use at a moment's notice. Begin using them, and use them often. Why not? Again, you deserve it. It is your life and your experience. Experiencing those high vibrating emotions will also create a ripple effect with those around you. You will begin to notice that the emotions of others around you are tending to be at a higher vibration as well, as you attract that. Congratulations, you will have just witnessed a most beautiful *law of the universe*, and how your emotions can create, attract, and impact others through their ripple effect.

So, let's take a look at this. Not only can you raise your vibration and experience bringing more love and joy to yourself, you also create a ripple effect in sharing it with others, who can, in turn, share it back with you. This can create a very wonderful cycle of the sharing of beautiful high vibrating emotions rather than sharing the opposite. This can assist you in changing and letting go of old patterns that do not feel good to you. As you replace the old patterns with new patterns of sharing what <u>does</u> feel good to you, you are creating a cycle that feels good and is healthy for you and everyone around you.

Focus on how often you wish to reward yourself and which reward you want to experience next. Incorporate a more formal meditation when you wish, for a specific purpose, but it is not necessary to follow a strict regimen to experience the rewards of simple meditations or simple pleasures each day. It is always up to you and what you wish to experience. When a meditation becomes a burden or an unwanted obligation, there are low vibrating emotions attached. That is not what you want to create. Notice what works for you. If you desire *quiet time* at the end of your day, as you are not finding this time during your day, then choose a simple meditation at the end of the day to get you started. If you wish to choose a more formal meditation to *experience* what it is like, that can be very helpful to teach you in understanding and noticing the difference.

Remember, when you enjoy a meditation, what you're choosing to do is to set aside time for your pleasure. Again, you deserve it. It can be interesting to take notes after a meditation or document your experience in a journal. It does not have to be a book, just notes. This can allow you to look back and notice how this experience has assisted you with your growth and in your creations. You have the opportunity to notice what is working so that you can become even more creative.

The more you connect with your Divine source and the frequencies of the "Rays of Light," the greater *your* connection grows. You may find that in time you connect more quickly with the Angels or your guides. Are you are paying attention and listening to the guidance throughout the day, and has that now become your new pattern? Congratulations, you have just created a new pattern for yourself. That is exactly how it works.

Your opportunities to create are unlimited as this universe is vast and has no limitations. You can shed any number of old patterns such as believing in the myth that you are limited in what you can do, or thinking in your mental mind that your boss is holding you back from success, or the old pattern of thinking that others in society are stopping you from living your dreams. It is truly up to you, as you were each born with free will, no matter who you are.

Mediation allows you to experience your dreams in real time, right now, or anytime that you wish, not just when you are sleeping. Dreaming and believing is creation. Creation is growth. Growth leads to understanding, remembering, and living your life in your physical body with more pleasure and joy, the way that you were meant to live.

Meditation allows you the opportunity to *have it all*. There are no restrictions to *having it all*. Everyone can choose this no matter what your background, your color, what neighborhood you live in, or what education you do or do not have. A "Rays of Light" Meditation is more than meditation; it is a remembrance, understanding, and information on *how it works*. It is much simpler than you can ever imagine.

Use your imagination, be a child and let go of the restrictions that you have been taught. Those restrictions are not truth; they are illusions which are keeping you from the truth, your growth, and remembrance.

It is time for you to create your own definition of meditation. This chapter has given you an outline and some information on meditation. The formal meditations in the following chapter, Chapter 8, will get you started. You can work with the more formal meditations, simple meditations, or both. You can also add a mantra (a high vibrating sound or tone) or a short sequence of high vibrating sounds, to your meditations. Please experiment. The focus of the formal meditations in this book, however, will specifically be using *only* the vibrations of the "Rays of Light."

Remember to practice meditation often. When you think about it as enjoyment and pleasure, rather than a need to follow an exact schedule, you can begin to enjoy it and experience the results very quickly. You can set aside time consistently and regularly if that feels good to you or you can be sporadic if that is what feels good. This is your creation. It is important to remember to include time for yourself each day, however that works for you. Once you begin to reap the benefits and receive the rewards of your creations, you may look forward to setting aside a certain time for yourself each day, just for you.

It is all up to you and your choices, as always. And again, the outcome is your choice. Do you want to choose pleasure, joy, and love, or the opposite? Think about it, as these choices will never go away. They will always be front and center for you.

Create or use meditations that are perfect for you, and bring joy to yourself and to others. What you experience, you share, and what you share creates a ripple effect. We are all in this together, so to speak, and that includes the entire universe, not just the planet of Earth.

Chapter Eight
Illuminating the Darkness

Chapter Eight: Illuminating the Darkness

The following meditations are intended to bring in the frequencies of the "Rays of Light" which will assist you in balancing the light and dark and in bringing in light, love, and remembrance. The "Rays of Light" assist you in receiving clear communication, remembrance, balance, and with a better focus for you to better *listen to the dark*, and to hear the guidance. They assist you in connecting with your Divine Source, the Angels, and your guides. The "Rays of Light" illuminate "all that is" and shed light, so to speak, on darkness. The "Rays of Light" carry frequencies, Angels, and loving beings that can assist you with your vibrations, especially the vibrations that you are working on for the purpose of your growth.

The "Rays of Light" meditations can also be used for cleansing, healing, balancing, and re-aligning your chakras, and can feel very calming. This calming can assist you in *letting go* of the chatter in your head. Each time you access and receive the "Rays of Light," you slowly deepen your connection with your Divine Source and "all that is," and also your connection to Mother Earth. Your growth will be supported and you will receive assistance and guidance. Be sure to pay attention for signs and the guidance.

The "Rays of Light" meditations can be used for the purpose of a general type of healing on all levels, in the physical and non-physical. You can add a mantra or tones to the meditations if you wish to increase the vibrations. You can also add a special intention for creating something new in your life, to assist you in letting go of old patterns, to assist you with a particular situation, or to assist you with your physical body.

Archangel Michael is asked to assist in the "Guidance and Healing Meditation." Archangel Michael carries very high frequencies that allow Him to easily assist you with these tasks. You can also ask your Divine Source. If you wish to choose another Angel or guide, you can experiment to see the difference in how it feels. Be sure that you are asking for assistance from a Divine being that will bring in the highest of frequencies for the greatest outcome.

This chapter contains two meditations, and two versions of each meditation. One version is written in *second person* while the other version is written in *first person*. The two versions allow you to choose the version that feels more comfortable for you, whether you are using it for yourself or sharing it with another.

The "Guidance Meditation" is meant to channel the frequencies of the "Rays of Light" to assist you in clear communication and the guidance from your Divine Source, the Angels, and your guides, which can support your personal growth on all levels. General healing benefits are also included.

The "Healing and Guidance Meditation" is used to access the frequencies of the "Rays of Light" to assist you with general healing benefits, special intentions (including special healing intentions), and a more elevated and deeper connection with "all that is," including Mother Earth. This meditation serves to assist you in clear communication and the guidance from your Divine Source, the Angels, and your guides, which can support your personal growth on all levels. Following step five in this meditation you can include your special intention, if you have one, before moving to step six. Putting any intention in writing can greatly increase the benefit and the result of that intention.

You can receive information in many ways from your Divine Source, the Angels, and your guides. Information may come in the form of thoughts, words, images, or through any of your senses or emotions. Just allow and accept them, taking notice of everything. It is all information and everything has meaning. Remember, everything is energy. You may want to take notes of your experience and the information and messages that you receive to maintain a record. The information does not always make sense at the time, however, later (possibly an hour, a day, or month later) it may become clear and it may make perfect sense. It is like putting together the pieces of a puzzle. There is a whole picture after completion; it is one puzzle piece leading to another, like a treasure hunt. If you look at the information with curiosity (a high vibrating emotion) and approach it with a sense of fun (another high vibrating emotion), it can be very exciting and rewarding.

Are you ready? Only you can answer that question. You are each ready in your own time and space. Some of you may not choose to participate at all. That is the beauty of free will. The choice is always up to you. If you don't like the result, you can make a different choice. You are the creator.

"Rays of Light" Guidance Meditation: In Second Person

You may sit in any position that is comfortable to you. If you feel that you need more grounding, you may sit in a chair with your back straight and your feet flat on the ground.

1. Visualize roots growing from the bottom of your feet, extending into the center and core of Mother Earth. Visualize wrapping the roots around a beautiful crystal (of your choosing) as an anchor.
2. Ask for protection. Ask all loving beings of the "Rays of Light" to surround you with a veil of love and protection during this meditation, in the physical and non-physical, on all levels and in all time and space. Ask for this veil to allow only the highest of vibrations, releasing all else, with love, grace, and gratitude.
3. Close your eyes and ask for your Divine Source, the Angels, your guides, Mother Earth, your higher self, and all loving beings of the "Rays of Light" to assist with this

meditation and to fill you with the frequencies of the "Rays of Light" and "all that is." You may ask any being from the Divine realm to assist in this meditation.

4. Ask for the "Rays of Light" to enter your highest chakra, above your Crown Chakra, and then to enter into your Crown Chakra, sweeping down into your Root Chakra, through your grounding cord, into Mother Earth giving love, gratitude, and appreciation to Mother Earth and all She does.

5. Ask to be provided guidance and communication and to receive this with clarity and openness and with truth and remembrance. Feel that you are open and worthy of receiving with love, grace, and gratitude.

6. Ask for the "Rays of Light" to enter your highest chakra above your Crown Chakra, and then enter into your Crown Chakra. Ask the "Rays of Light" to expand, and to cleanse, heal, balance, and re-align all of your chakras, every cell in your body, and your entire aura, and to fill your body with love, grace, gratitude, and remembrance of "all that is." Ask to be brought into harmony and balance with love and remembrance, light and darkness, and "all that is." Allow yourself a moment to experience the frequencies and energies.

7. Ask to connect with your Divine Source, the Angels, and your guides, and your higher self at this time. Listen to your etheric (spiritual) heart and let go of any thoughts related to your mental mind. If you are mentally thinking

about anything, release those thoughts and allow the thoughts and images from your etheric (spiritual) heart to flow in gently and with love as you receive them. Do not put forth effort to think in any way. Open yourself up to hear, see, know, feel, experience, and to understand in a way that is perfect for you. Ask to receive clear guidance now, throughout the day, and when you lay down to rest at night. Ask for assistance and to be open to receiving "all that is" and to easily recognize and understand the guidance. Acknowledge that you are deserving of receiving this love and guidance with clarity. Maintain this connection for as long as you wish.

8. Please remember to give thanks to your Divine Source, the Angels, your guides, your higher self, Mother Earth, and all loving beings of the "Rays of Light" that have assisted you in this meditation.

9. Take whatever time you wish to sit in peace and harmony with this beautiful connection.

"Rays of Light" Guidance Meditation: In First Person

You may sit in any position that is comfortable. If you feel that you need more grounding, you may sit in a chair with your back straight and your feet flat on the ground.

1. I visualize roots growing from the bottom of my feet, extending into the center and core of Mother Earth. I visualize wrapping the roots around a beautiful crystal

as an anchor. I see a beautiful crystal (of my choosing) as my anchor.

2. I ask for protection. I ask all loving beings of the "Rays of Light" to surround me with a veil of love and protection during this meditation, in the physical and non-physical, on all levels, and in all time and space. I ask for this veil to allow only the highest of vibrations, releasing all else, with love, grace, and gratitude.

3. I close my eyes and ask for my Divine Source, the Angels, my guides, Mother Earth, my higher self, and all loving beings of the "Rays of Light" to assist with this meditation and to fill me with the frequencies of the "Rays of Light" and "all that is." I ask (any being from the Divine realm) to assist in this meditation.

4. I ask for the "Rays of Light" to enter my highest chakra, above my Crown Chakra, and then to enter into my Crown Chakra, sweeping down into my Root Chakra, through my grounding cord, into Mother Earth giving love, gratitude, and appreciation to Mother Earth and all She does.

5. I ask to be provided guidance and communication and to receive this with clarity and openness and with truth and remembrance. I am open and worthy of receiving with love, grace, and gratitude.

6. I ask for the "Rays of Light" to enter my highest chakra above my Crown Chakra, and then enter into my Crown Chakra. I ask the "Rays of Light" to expand, and to cleanse, heal, balance, and re-align all of my chakras,

every cell in my body, and my entire aura and to fill my body with love, grace, gratitude, and remembrance of "all that is." I ask to be brought into harmony and balance with love and remembrance, light and darkness, and "all that is." I allow myself a moment to experience the frequencies and energies.

7. I wish to connect with my Divine Source, the Angels, and my guides, and my higher self at this time. I listen to my etheric (spiritual) heart and I let go of any thoughts related to my mental mind. If I am mentally thinking about anything, I release those thoughts and allow the thoughts and images from my etheric (spiritual) heart to flow in gently and with love as I receive them. I do not put forth effort to think in any way. I open myself up to hear, see, know, feel, experience, and to understand in a way that is perfect for me. I ask to receive clear guidance now, throughout the day and when I lay down to rest at night. I ask for assistance and to be open to receiving "all that is" and to easily recognize and understand the guidance. I acknowledge that I am deserving of receiving this love and guidance with clarity. I maintain this connection for as long as I wish.

8. I give appreciation and gratitude to my Divine Source, the Angels, my guides, my higher self, Mother Earth, and all loving beings of the "Rays of Light" that have assisted me in this meditation.

9. I sit in peace and harmony with this beautiful connection.

"Rays of Light" Healing and Guidance Meditation: In Second Person

You may sit in any position that is comfortable to you. If you feel that you need more grounding, you may sit in a chair with your back straight and your feet flat on the ground.

1. Visualize roots growing from the bottom of your feet, extending into the center and core of Mother Earth. Visualize wrapping the roots around a beautiful crystal (of ·your choosing) as an anchor.
2. Ask for protection. Ask all loving beings of the "Rays of Light" to surround you with a veil of love and protection during this meditation, in the physical and non-physical, on all levels, and in all time and space. Ask for this veil to allow only the highest of vibrations, releasing all else, with love, grace, and gratitude.
3. Close your eyes and ask for your Divine Source, the Angels, your guides, Mother Earth, your higher self, and all loving beings of the "Rays of Light" to assist with this healing and meditation and to fill you with the "Rays of Light." You may ask any being from the Divine realm to assist in this meditation.
4. Ask to be provided "all that is" from the "Rays of Light." State that you are open and deserving of receiving this

love and these frequencies in the physical and non-physical, on all levels, and in all time and space.

5. Ask Archangel Michael to assist you with removing all in your aura that is not of the highest vibration, so that you experience only the highest frequencies and energies during this meditation. Ask Archangel Michael to remove any low vibrating impurities that are released by you during this meditation.

6. Ask for the "Rays of Light" to enter your highest chakra, above your Crown Chakra, and then to enter into your Crown Chakra, sweeping down into your Root Chakra, through your grounding cord, into Mother Earth giving love, gratitude, and appreciation to Mother Earth and all that She does.

7. Ask for a Divine violet filter to be placed below your feet to allow only the highest energies of Mother Earth to enter your body. Ask Mother Earth to run Her energies up through the violet filter, through your grounding cord, through your Root Chakra, and up through all of your chakras and your body, joining the frequencies of the "Rays of Light" for this meditation.

8. Ask for the "Rays of Light" to expand and to cleanse, heal, balance, and re-align all of your chakras, every cell in your body, and your entire aura, and to fill your entire body with love, grace, gratitude, and remembrance of "all that is." Allow yourself a moment to experience the frequencies and energies.

9. Ask for the "Rays of Light" to continue to infuse all of your chakras, every cell in your body, and your entire aura with unconditional love, brining you into harmony and balance with love and remembrance, light and darkness, and "all that is." Experience this for as long as you wish until you feel refreshed and rejuvenated.

10. Place your palms on your heart filling yourself with these loving frequencies and energies. This need only be done through your express intentions (your specific thoughts or words). Experience this for as long as you wish.

11. For a special intention, send, through your intentions, these loving frequencies and energies to any person, situation, special cause, relationship, or to anything that you desire. You can be very specific about a special or general intention, creating a beautiful experience, a fun vacation, attracting courage, aiding with physical discomfort, etc. Experience this for as long as you wish.

12. For those who wish to connect with your Divine Source, the Angels, your guides, and your higher self at this time: listen to your etheric (spiritual) heart, letting go of any thoughts related to your mental mind. If you are mentally thinking about anything, release those thoughts and allow the thoughts and images from your etheric (spiritual) heart to flow in gently and with love as you receive them. Do not put forth effort to think in any way. Open yourself up to hear, see, know, feel, experience, and to understand in a way that is perfect

for you. Ask to receive clear guidance now and throughout the day and when you lay down to rest at night. Ask for assistance and to be open to receiving "all that is" and to easily recognize and understand the guidance. Maintain this connection for as long as you wish.

13. When you have completed your meditation, please remember to give appreciation and gratitude to your Divine Source, the Angels (including Archangel Michael), your guides, Mother Earth, your higher self, and to all the loving beings of the "Rays of Light" that have assisted you in this meditation.

14. Take whatever time you wish to sit in peace and harmony with these beautiful frequencies and energies.

"Rays of Light" Healing and Guidance Meditation: In First Person

You may sit in any position that is comfortable to you. If you feel that you need more grounding, you may sit in a chair with your back straight and your feet flat on the ground.

1. I visualize roots growing from the bottom of my feet, extending into the center and core of Mother Earth. I visualize wrapping them around a beautiful crystal as an anchor. I see a beautiful crystal (of my choosing) as my anchor.

2. I ask for protection. I ask all loving beings of the "Rays of Light" to surround me with a veil of love and protection during this meditation, in the physical and non-physical, on all levels, and in all time and space. I ask for this veil to allow only the highest of vibrations, releasing all else, with love, grace, and gratitude.

3. I Close my eyes and ask for my Divine Source, the Angels, my guides, Mother Earth, my higher self, and all loving beings of the "Rays of Light" to assist in this meditation and to fill me with the "Rays of Light." I ask (any being from the Divine realm) to assist in this meditation.

4. I ask to be provided "all that is" from the "Rays of Light." I am open and deserving of receiving this love and these frequencies in the physical and non-physical, on all levels, and in all time and space.

5. I ask Archangel Michael to assist me in removing all in my aura that is not of the highest vibration, so that I experience only the highest frequencies and energies during this meditation. I ask Archangel Michael to remove any low vibrating impurities that are released by me during this meditation.

6. I ask for the "Rays of Light" to enter my highest chakra, above my Crown Chakra, and then to enter into my Crown Chakra, sweeping down into my Root Chakra, through my grounding cord, into Mother Earth. I give love, gratitude, and appreciation to Mother Earth and all that She does.

7. I ask for a Divine violet filter to be placed below my feet to allow only the highest energies of Mother Earth to enter my body. I ask Mother Earth to run these energies up through the violet filter, through your Root Chakra, and through all of your chakras and your body, joining the frequencies of the "Rays of Light" for this meditation.

8. I ask for the "Rays of Light" to expand and to cleanse, heal, balance, and re-align all of my chakras, every cell in my body, and my entire aura, and to fill my entire body with love, grace, gratitude, and remembrance of "all that is." I allow myself a moment to experience the frequencies and energies.

9. I ask for the "Rays of Light" to continue to infuse all my chakras, every cell in my body, and my entire aura with unconditional love, bringing me into harmony and balance with love and remembrance, light and darkness, and "all that is." I experience this for as long as I wish until I feel refreshed and rejuvenated.

10. I place my palms on my heart filling myself with these loving frequencies and energies. I do this through my express intentions (my specific thoughts or words). I experience this for as long as I wish.

11. For a special intention, I send, through my intentions, these loving frequencies and energies to any person, situation, special cause, relationship, or to anything that

I desire. I am very specific about a special or general intention, creating a beautiful experience, a fun vacation, attracting courage, aiding with physical discomfort, etc. I experience this for as long as I wish.

12. If I wish to connect with my Divine Source, the Angels, my guides, and my higher self at this time. I listen to my etheric (spiritual) heart, letting go of any thoughts related to my mental mind. If I am mentally thinking about anything, I release those thoughts and allow the thoughts and images from my etheric (spiritual) heart to flow in gently and with love as I receive them. I do not put forth effort to think in any way. I open myself up to hear, see, know, feel, experience, and to understand in a way that is perfect for me. I ask to receive clear guidance now and throughout the day and when I lay down to rest at night. I ask for assistance and to be open to receiving "all that is" and to easily recognize and understand the guidance. I maintain this connection for as long as I wish.

13. I give appreciation and gratitude to my Divine Source, the Angels (including Archangel Michael), my guides, to Mother Earth, my higher self, and to all loving beings of the "Rays of Light" that have assisted me in this meditation.

14. I take whatever time I wish to sit in peace and harmony with these beautiful frequencies and energies.

Now that you have practiced with some formal meditations, and have learned how they feel to you, this would be a good time for you to experiment. Create a meditation just for you. You can start with something short and simple. Pay attention to how it feels and be sure to remember the five guidelines recommended in Chapter 7 to be included in a meditation.

Chapter Nine
A Healing Journey

Chapter Nine: A Healing Journey

This title of this chapter, "A Healing Journey," emphasizes the truth that *to heal* is truly a journey. There are miracles for sure; however in many cases healing can be considered a personal process or a *journey* that occurs over time. Your physical and/or emotional discomforts tend to develop over time. In other words, they are created over time with unhealthy vibrations in the emotions that are attached to your thoughts, your words, and your actions. It takes time to reverse and change the results as you begin to understand and choose to create something different and to release the old. There is a process of understanding and learning to think, speak, and behave differently, as you let go of the old patterns and create and attract something new with high vibrating emotions.

Just as the emotions do not feel good while you are experiencing and creating physical or emotional discomfort, you may also notice that, the emotions may at times not feel good as you are healing and releasing the old patterns and low vibrating energies that were part of that creation. Low vibrating energies do not feel good whether you are creating or releasing them. However, releasing them with love can assist in elevating the vibration to feel better during that process. As you release the old patterns, this will allow room for your growth and for you to bring in the new patterns, and to attract new energies and frequencies with higher vibrations that feel more loving.

In order to begin any healing process, it is recommended that you let go of old patterns and your old way of thinking, speaking, and behaving that may carry low vibrating emotions. This is a very simple idea, yet it is not always easy to accomplish. Old habits and patterns are embedded into your body and can interfere with creating what you truly desire. First, you must recognize the old habits and patterns, and understand and acknowledge that they are your creation, so you can choose to let go. This is recognizing, acknowledging, understanding, and taking accountability in your creation. This is a first step to healing. As you choose to let go of the old, you can then choose new patterns that are supportive and uplifting of your desires.

Healing can be defined and viewed in many different ways. In this book, healing is not used in the traditional manner and has a very different definition. You will not find this definition in a journal, the medical community, or the dictionary. Healing can be seen as any of the following:

1. Recognition of a pattern or intention that is interfering with your true desires, and resulting in the opposite.
2. After recognition, accepting and taking accountability for a pattern or intention that is interfering with your true desires, and resulting in the opposite.
3. Taking a small step to choose a new word, a new thought or a new action, which attaches a very high

vibrating emotion, and brings about a result that is uplifting and feels good to you and to others.

4. Recognizing and acknowledging that you have a choice in how you feel and taking action to create what feels good to you and to others.

5. Paying attention and <u>taking action</u> with your true guidance to care for yourself by scheduling an appointment with your Doctor regarding an ailment, attending a Yoga or Qi Gong class, or exercise class for energy, going for a walk for peace and calm, spending time in nature to rejuvenate, listening to soft comforting music for relaxation, following a suggestion to take a vacation (taking an hour or two or a few days), using meditations to access guidance to *feel better*, or accessing the "Rays of Light" for any positive purpose. These are only a few examples.

6. Choosing to feel and experience a higher vibrating emotion such as joy or happiness when you wake up in the morning and continuing to choose that experience and that emotion throughout the day or when you go to bed at night.

There is more that can be added to this definition but this will give you the idea. Healing involves much more than a result that you can see and experience in a physical sense. It includes a different way of *seeing* and understanding how the result was created and it includes taking accountability for that creation. It also includes taking actions, including small steps, to release that which you have created as you begin to create that which you desire. It is that simple.

Also know that some of you may have chosen to come into this world with a specific ailment, or malfunction in your body. If this was chosen by you, as part of your life experience here on this planet, know that is part of your experience or lesson. If this is what was chosen, it is for the purpose of understanding and learning to live in your physical body with whatever you have chosen. Part of your healing journey may then involve accepting and living with an uplifting vibration regardless of what you have chosen for your physical body, as acceptance is the first step to healing. Remember, you were born with blinders on, in darkness, so do not expect to remember making these choices.

You can use visualization to assist you in the process of letting go of the old. An example would be to picture vibrations and how they must look. See the low vibrating emotions as dark sludge, layering itself around and within you. Each layer gets heavier and darker with weight. As you carry the extra weight around you become less mobile, feeling more sluggish and begin to sink deeper into the old patterns and just plain not feeling good. You are stuck.

Visualize choosing something different that is of a higher vibration. Visualize yourself washing off the old that appears as sludge. Wash this sludge with love and the frequencies of the "Rays of Light" as you choose to say *no* to the old patterns. Bathe yourself in the emotions of joy. See yourself choosing high vibrating emotions and choosing new patterns. Watch how the sludge melts away and notice the change in the weighted feeling. Notice the experience as the heaviness is released, allowing you to feel lightened and refreshed. Watch how it feels as you free yourself from the heavy ties of the old patterns.

This process of releasing will make space for the new. Make space for the positive by letting go of the opposite, the old patterns, and releasing the low vibrating emotions. Allow room for the new to step in, always with love, dignity, and respect. Allow room for love and joy into your heart, never the opposite. Fill yourself with respect and dignity that is for both you and for others. These words and thoughts carry high vibrating emotions, especially when they are paired with the emotion of love. Always check in with yourself to see how it *feels*.

It is important to honor and respect yourself as you focus on staying in the flow and your desire to heal and to create what feels good and uplifting to you. You have been provided information and meditations in this book (Chapter 8) to assist you in understanding *how it works*. You are provided with the steps to healing sessions for cleansing, healing, balancing, and re-aligning your chakras (Chapters 11 and 12).

For example, take a look at how you might be creating something, unknowingly, that does not feel good. As has been presented, low vibrating emotions can impact your chakras in creating sluggish or slow feelings and movement. In turn that can impact your physical body and your health. Take a close look at <u>drama</u> as a vibration. Drama, often times, has low vibrating emotions attached. Drama can also be easily disguised, coming with the appearance of being healthy. Do not be fooled or drawn in by drama of low vibrations.

Know that when drama presents itself in yourself and in others, it is O.K. to take a step away, with kindness in your heart. Be aware that when you are stepping away from low vibrating emotions of drama in yourself, you must also remember to step away from the emotions of low vibrating drama presented by others. This is healing.

As an example, one type of this drama may be the repetition of low vibrating actions, thoughts, or words, in the form of complaining. It might take the form of a person expressing *neediness* by repeatedly asking for *help*, over and over, when they are choosing to not take actions of change or to assist themselves. Drama may appear in another who is sharing their very low vibrating emotions in a low vibrating story, repeated this over and over again, to maybe attract sympathy or attention. Drama may be a disguise when it is truly the emotion of *neediness* in desiring attention.

These emotions with low vibrations are often times accompanied by a lack of willingness of another to try something new, to make any changes in their thoughts or behavior to attract in a positive way. Or it may be seen in a lack of willingness to make a plan of action to move forward with a resolution. This can be witnessed as a lack of willingness to consider personal accountability in a creation. There is often times blaming and judgment of others that accompanies this type of drama. This again, brings in very low vibrations. This pattern is not healthy for the person repeating the pattern or the person providing a low vibrating response such as sympathy (sympathy is different from empathy) and supporting blaming or judgment. None of these vibrations feel good, do they?

Say *yes* to dignity and respect as you honor yourself and others. You can respect others in their choice of patterns, without judgment, and at the same time you can remember to live your choice, not the choice of another. You can live your choice of high vibrating emotions, while you step away from another's choice, without judgment or blaming. This is love, and radiates a most beautiful vibration that has a ripple effect on all. Trust and believe this as you step away. This is healing.

When you choose to step away from another's drama and live without the weight of low vibrating emotions, you are supporting your growth while you allow an opportunity for another to make their choice to grow or not. Give love to yourself and to others, while you let go of the old pattern of feeling obligated to living another's choice or to an obligation to support low vibrating emotions such as sympathy, judgment, or blame. Allow others to choose just as you allow yourself to also choose. You have a choice. Every person has *free will*. Choose to live your choice and give gratitude for the experience and the opportunity for your growth. Do not look back. Do not re-live the old patterns again, whether they are your patterns or the patterns of others. This is healing.

When you live your choices for growth and experience, you are then offering an example for others as they witness your choice and your results. Support others by living your choice and living it with the vibration of love. Support others with love and hope, not the opposite. This is healing.

You may be asking, "How might I do that?" How do you turn a complaint into a resolution, since complaining is an emotion that carries a very low vibration? If another comes to you with a complaint, simply listen and respond with empathy (not sympathy) and understanding. You can point out options with kindness in your heart. You can choose not to participate in the complaint and choose words of a high vibration to uplift the conversation, without blame or judgment.

There are ways to offer positive support without supporting the low vibration. You can re-direct another with your words and thoughts carrying emotions of a high vibration. You might re-direct another by saying, "So what is your plan? What is your next step? How do you want to move forward? What would you like to choose to feel better? Is there something I can do to assist you in the resolution?"

You can offer assistance, for example, by offering to assist them in a move, in making a meal, or in giving someone aid in cleaning their house, or their yard. Give your support and empathy in this manner. Do not accept low vibrating emotions. You do not have to live with another's choice to simply complain. Accept information and give information, not complaints. Information and knowledge carry high vibrating emotions. Complaining carries low vibrating emotions.

Remained focused on providing positive information and knowledge rather than adding to the low vibrating emotions carried with a complaint or judgment. You can *go to the light* and *ask your Angels* for assistance. Choose your thoughts, your words, and your approach with high vibrating emotions. Assist others by re-directing their thoughts (as you re-direct your own thoughts), with the high vibrations of love, empathy, respect, understanding, and support. Walk away from the low vibrations of sympathy, blame, and judgment. This is healing.

Create a ripple effect by saying "No thank-you." to complaining or low vibrating drama. Change the vibration by choosing a plan or a resolution and encouraging the same with others. You may choose to say, "I see you are not ready for a plan or a resolution. Take the time you need to look at that and we can talk more when you wish to create, a plan, or a resolution. I would love to support your plan, your resolution, or support a positive approach that will assist you." Offer any high vibrating thought to support high vibrating emotions rather than supporting the opposite. This is supporting growth and healing for you and for another. This is healing.

Re-direct another coming to you with a low vibration and *stick to your choice*. Honor yourself as you honor and respect others. Do not get caught in the old pattern of clinging onto or supporting another's low vibrating choice, and feeling the need to be sympathetic. The emotions of neediness and sympathy carry very low vibrating emotions that do not support healing or growth. Offer support in a loving way with high vibrating choices. Start with a little step. Little steps start you on your way to growth; little steps quickly turn into big steps.

Remember to *live* your example; do not back down to satisfy another's expectation of you. Be that beacon of light. Show others how it's done. Let them see an example in you. Choose no judgment, just the simple awareness, with honor and respect for everyone as you wash away the low vibrations. This is healing.

There is no need to argue. Arguments create very low vibrating emotions. There is no right or wrong, only choices. Exercise your *free will* as you teach others how to exercise their *free will*. Be an example by using your *will*. Remember, your *will* is incredibly strong and very, very powerful. You were born with this *will* and it rightfully belongs to you. Your *will* creates and it can also release, heal, and change patterns.

Your *will* is very magical, and it is your choice. Your *will* does not belong to anyone else, unless you choose to give it away. Do not give away your *free will* and your choices. Again, that is your choice. Your *free will* is a gift from the Divine, your Divine Source. You were each born with this beautiful gift. Exercise your *will* and teach others how to do the same. This is healing.

Pay close attention to the obsession of repeating your own thoughts and your own stories. There is often a human tendency to repeat thoughts or tell your story over and over again. Does that story, those thoughts or those words carry emotions of a high vibration or the opposite? This is a vibration you are creating and sending out to the universe; you will surely attract it back. Notice when you are repeating a story. Does the story have a good ending, for example? Is the emotion one of joy? Does the story carry emotions of doubt in yourself or are you looking for others to reward you, acknowledge you, or validate you in your not so comforting emotions? If you are to repeat a word or thought, you want it to be with an emotion of the highest vibration possible to attract back the same, one of confidence, respect, dignity, knowledge, and information.

Are you listening to another who is repeating thoughts, words, and stories over and over again? This is an emotion with a vibration that you are participating in. Pay close attention to the emotions attached to these vibrations. Is another sharing with you with you their medical concern by way of providing information and instructions with love and respect, which are high vibrating emotions? Is another repeating stories of unhappiness filled with judgment, anger, or blame? These carry very low vibrations.

This is when you must look closer and determine if this vibration of the emotion is uplifting for you and the other person or is it the opposite? Do you want to be bound in the cement of low vibrations that weigh you down or would you like to be uplifted and freed by high vibrating emotions of love, assistance, and support? The choice is yours.

Your *will* is so very powerful. You choose how you want to use your *will*. Remember to always express your *free will* with love, gratitude, and appreciation. Yes, you can express gratitude for the recognition of these patterns. You can express and feel grateful to those that have presented to you low vibrations allowing you to choose and to grow. Your awareness and understanding allows you to look at others and situations more closely and see your opportunities for growth. Your awareness allows you to choose to create something different while you are being a shining an example, a beacon of light, to others. That is a very beautiful gift to be grateful for. This is healing.

It may appear to be more of a challenge when it is another who chooses to repeatedly share their words and actions that are with emotions of a low vibration. They may come from a family member or a friend. You may feel that you have an obligation to listen, out of love, or out of politeness or guilt, as that is what you have been taught. Remember to look again at the emotions that are attached. Love does not carry a high vibration when there is the low vibration in the emotion of guilt attached, for example.

Stepping away with love will move you to a place that allows you to intend pure love, for yourself and others, which is the highest of the vibrations. Step away. It is O.K to say *no* to being drawn into another's pattern that does not carry emotions with high vibrations. You are accountable for yourself. Support and honor others by respecting their choices. Also, respect your choice to say *no*, with love, and let go of old patterns, allowing opportunities for growth for both of you. Let go of the old patterns. This is healing.

You can offer assistance in supporting the plan of another. Do not choose to support complaining; choose to support a plan, a resolution or assistance in a positive manner. Remember, "What's your plan?" Be creative as you respond. What is a resolution, or what will allow one to see their resolution? It may be time for a walk in the park, sitting in nature, exercise, meditation, listening to music, or pitching in to assist in a positive way, if possible. There is the start to a plan. It may be a perfect time to quiet one's self.

Choosing a high vibrating emotion in your response to an unhealthy repetition would be the relief and the start of a plan. This can create a spark of excitement and hope which can be soothing and calming, allowing and promoting emotions of belief, trust, and relief, or a peaked interest in the *next step* to take. These words and thoughts carry high vibrating emotions, as does curiosity, all of which can elevate your thoughts and ideas to move to action steps of growth, in a positive and healthy way. This is healing.

Your *healing journey* can be assisted by choosing a special intention that can be included in the "Healing and Guidance Meditation" in Chapter 8. You would choose the same intention to be repeated in this meditation over a period of five days. You can choose a special intention during the meditation to attract higher frequencies and accelerated growth, in a specific area.

This assistance in your *healing journey* would be accomplished by completing the "Healing and Guidance Meditation" two times per day, once in the morning and once in the evening, for a period of five days. This totals 10 meditations, five days in a row, including the same specific intention included each time. Allow the frequencies and energies to continue to flow and be patient as you wait for your results. Remember, the universe is very large and it takes time to release what has been created. Stay your course, remain positive, and do not change your focus.

There are many steps to each healing process and healing can come in many different forms. It can often times come in little steps such as a referral to a doctor, by an introduction to someone that can later assist you with a business need, an opportunity for a job interview that you have been desiring, the beginning of therapy or chiropractic sessions that can assist your body in the healing process. You must give this process time.

After the meditations are complete, pay very close attention to the guidance as healing comes in many different forms. Follow all guidance that is received, and maintain high vibrating emotions such as trust, belief, and faith, knowing that your intention has been sent to the universe, creating the perfect resolution for you. Do not stray from attaching the high vibration emotions to your intention or you may change your intention to another direction and a different result. Relax and know you are creating the perfect result, allowing days, weeks, or maybe months for the universe to complete the most wonderful ending.

A personal note from the author, Linda, about her healing journey:

I, Linda Street, received clear guidance to share in these pages some of my personal experiences about my healing journey. As I have learned to ask for guidance, I have learned to better recognize and to trust and follow the guidance. This information is not going to involve relating anything dramatic or *attention getting*; it is simply truth from my heart to yours.

I began to experiment with energy many years ago, as I took courses and received certifications. I learned that no path was a wrong path; my paths took twists and turns depending upon my choices. I found that I can take a long path with great difficulty or I can take a shorter path with more freedom and enjoyment. The more I trusted and believed, the more I grew to understand and to learn how energy truly works. The more I learned, the more I appreciated life and enjoyed myself.

Living in a world where I grew up learning and believing in so many unhealthy patterns, I always knew in my heart that something was not right. It did not make sense for me to so often feel unworthy and unloved. As I learned to listen to my heart, understand the guidance and yes, to follow the guidance, I have validated that my feelings all along were correct.

As I began to look at this picture and to learn without judgment, I could see that it was all part of the path that I had chosen. I began to let go, one by one, of the heart aches, the fears, the disbelief in myself, and the lack of confidence in myself that I had previously accepted as truth. As I continued down my path, and as I let go of each and every belief that did not resonate as truth, or did not feel right for me, I learned the real meaning of truth. That was a key for me, knowing that the truth is what resonates in myself, not in what others think of me. The next step was to live that truth and let go of what others think of me.

As I live that truth, today my life is very different. I know that it is I who makes the choice. It is I who chooses happiness and love as often as I can, and I wish the same for others. I continue to remind myself each and every day to ask and to listen, to let go of judgment, and to choose a path that is in the flow of everything that feels good. These reminders and my desire to continue to learn and to *live* my beliefs will always be present in my life until my last physical breath. However, the difference is in the result. The difference is in living a more loving life with freedom from the past and with joy and admiration for the beauty that I am honored to experience every day. Freedom never felt so good.

I have received guidance to share with you some of my personal results as I was learning and understanding more about energy and the results that I can create. I began to experiment in simple ways with energy and continued to find new experiments since I loved the results. Later I began to experiment in bigger ways.

I retired in September, 2013 from a Human Resources position, working for a large corporation for over 15 years. Over those years, I often worked very long hours. It was not uncommon for me to ignore health issues and to choose to ignore needed appointments with my doctors. I believed that I was too busy to take the time and that it was my responsibility to complete my work as expected since that is what was important. At that time, if I needed to take off more than a day or two due to illness or needed to attend a doctor's appointment, I was questioned or could hear the sigh and the silence on the other end of the phone from my manager. So for a long time I avoided using the time that I was entitled to take as part of my health benefits.

 Escalating health concerns eventually forced me begin to honor myself, by taking time for my health, and by scheduling those appointments. It still took some time to release the guilt. As I honored myself, I recognized that it was time to take care of myself now since the health concerns that I ignored were not going away, and they were growing bigger. As I did so, I noticed changes. I noticed that my time off for appointments or my personal needs was being supported. I noticed that my wishes and intentions were being supported. It's about time I was thinking, not yet fully recognizing that it was I who created the change by honoring myself and my personal needs.

In 2013, I decided to correct my work/life balance. As I sat over the phone, in a discussion with my two managers regarding my upcoming goals in my position for the year, I decided to add one more goal. That goal was to work a 40 hour work week. I also added that I would be taking my one hour lunch every day, and that I would no longer be answering my emails and my work phone during lunch. I normally worked hours over the 40 hours required since I had been overwhelmed with emails and phone calls during the years that I had been working there, and had communicated that often in passing. I also normally answered emails and phone calls while squeezing in lunch. I expected to be this busy, as after all, I worked in Human Resources.

My new goals, thoughts and beliefs were readily supported by my two managers. I created several written affirmations for myself to support my goals. My affirmations involved intentions of my work day being very balanced, with my emails, phone calls, and projects being received in a very balanced way. I also asked for any needs for my Human Resource assistance to be requested and to come to me in a very balanced way. I asked for my days at work to be very balanced. And, of course, I always asked for a positive and fair resolution to every situation where I assisted.

As I focused each day on my affirmations, I noticed the difference in what I had been expecting and believing all of these years while working in a Human Resources position. I believed it was not possible to work in this role without working long hours each day. I always expected my emails and phone calls would be overwhelming. I expected to be *crazy busy* as I used to say. When asked in passing how I was doing I noticed that I would typically respond, "Great, but of course I am very busy and working lots of hours." So I changed the way that I thought about my position and the way that I responded to those questions. My response became very positive and an affirmation of what I now desired and expected. I would hear laughter as I responded, "Everything is wonderful. I am in the flow."

As I continued to follow my goals, I stood firm in the 40 hours, and stepped away from my desk at lunch, so as to not answer the phone or the emails. I noticed a complete change in two weeks. My emails and phone calls were balanced, as were the projects that I received and the requests for my assistance. My work day had become very balanced, and I was able to accomplish my work, meet the expectations of my job each day, and still meet my goals, within my 8 hour work day.

If this had been suggested as possible the year before, I never would have believed it. I watched as overwhelming phone calls and emails landed with those saying, "I am crazy busy" and they believed it to be true. Overwhelming projects landed with those who believed that part of the role in Human Resources was to take up the work for their Human Resource partners, rather than setting boundaries with their partners. I found this all to be very interesting.

As long as I stuck to my goals, everything stayed in balance. If I decided to alter my goal, just this one time, I noticed the difference. The energy and reflection showed up very quickly. Within two weeks of announcing my new goal, and living my goal, I was living the work life balance that I had been wanting for many years and I was still able to meet all expectations. That was amazing to me. I recognized all along that I had the *will* to make this change. This is just one of many examples from my own life.

As I continued to trust and believe, I decided in 2013 to take that trust a step further. Up until that time, I had been working part time with energies and the frequencies of the rays, offering teachings, presentations, and healing sessions. I decided to leave the security of a corporate job to do what I loved most, working with energies and the frequencies of the "Rays of Light" as a full time job. I decided to do what was in my heart. In other words, I chose to believe in myself, and to trust in the guidance that I had been receiving. I knew that I was working with very powerful frequencies that were to be shared and taught to others. I knew that I needed to share this knowledge in a book. I trusted this to be true.

So I left my Human resources job in September, 2013 and

continued on my path. My sole focus was on working with and teaching about the "Rays of Light." I had chosen to live it as best I had learned. As you know, living it is ongoing and includes reminders and practice every day.

During the writing of this book, I still have a couple of chapters left to complete and I have already begun to prepare for the classes that I will be offering, "Rays of Light" - Elevate Your Divine Connection." I have already completed the agenda for the two and one half day course. I was guided to go to a particular store one day and found the perfect materials for the class. I found a totally unexpected item that was perfect for the exercises in the course. I was thrilled. In fact, to date, I already have quite a few individuals that have expressed their sincere interest in completing the course.

This book will be self-published. I have two presentations scheduled later this year (2014,) June and August, to discuss the "Rays of Light," this book, and to hold book signings. I have not yet completed the book. This scheduling of events prior to completing this book demonstrates others trusting and believing in me as well as me, trusting and believing in myself. I am preparing for an Open House to introduce this book and I know that it will work out beautifully. It is I who will determine the details and pull it together. There is no sponsor, no one to advertise for me, and no one to promote me. It is only me, but a very powerful me, since I now know the secret. That is trust and belief. As long as I continue to ask for guidance, and then listen and to follow the guidance, trust and believe with all of my heart, everything will easily and perfectly fall into place and I will receive any assistance that I need and desire. And I know that, often times, the result will be even better than I expected.

I attended a workshop a couple of years ago with a focus on creating a power statement to share with others, that is representative of me. I walked away from that workshop with the power statement that I felt was perfect for me. The statement is, **"It's your heart, own it."** This was something that I needed to learn and I must continue to practice as I remind myself each day and share the message with others. Reach into your heart for the truth, as the truth will not let you down. Your heart knows the truth; trust it, believe it and own it. Do not give your truth away to anyone.

You and I are no different; we are on this journey together. We each are choosing our own paths, in our own time that is perfect for each of us. I wish you only the best and send to you the highest vibrations of love, honor, and respect.

Thank-you for assisting me on my journey.

Chapter Ten
A "How To" for the "Rays of Light"

Chapter Ten: A "How To" for the "Rays of Light"

The "Rays of Light" – A Healing Modality was introduced in June of 2013, when Linda Street was gifted with the teachings of the "Rays of Light." This modality includes a set of practices and movements that assist in channeling the frequencies of the "Rays of Light," and is used for a variety of intentions. This modality is shared in Chapters 11 and 12. The "Rays of Light" can be accessed for the purpose of chakra cleansing, healing, balancing, and re-alignment, for special intentions, for general healing and growth, and for assistance in the form of guidance from your Divine Source, the Angels, and your guides, to list a few examples.

There are many persons currently working with a variety of beautiful healing modalities, practices, and approaches, energies, frequencies, and rays. They each have a purpose and each of you is drawn to the perfect energies, frequencies, or practice that is perfect for you at any given time. There are also many persons sharing their beautiful gifts and their ability to access information, providing guidance, and simply providing love and assistance to others.

 The purpose of Linda's gift is to bring in the teachings of the "Rays of Light" from another realm. It is to bring in clarification and truth about the rays, which are "all that is," and to teach how each of you can access these rays. These frequencies, the information, and the practices are for those of you that feel drawn to it and have a belief and trust that it is perfect for you at this time. There are always many beautiful options from which you each can choose.

Not all questions about the "Rays of Light," the frequencies, and energy can or will be answered in this book. This book is meant to serve as an introduction, to offer information, and to answer some of your many questions. There will always be more to learn. Generating more questions and your curiosity is a good place to start. Learning to *listen to the dark* will assist you with more answers and information.

There is much more than meets the eye with the "Rays of Light." It is a healing modality for sure, but is also much more. The "all that is" covers it all. The 13 "Rays of Light" and all of the infinite rays and their frequencies, and of course the Angels assigned to each ray, can not only be used for the guidance, but also for general healing, growth, and for special intentions.

The "Rays of Light" can be used for the purpose of bringing in information, assistance, and guidance with the *ways of the Universe*, especially on this earth at this time. The "Rays of Light" are packed full of answers and information when you take a close look and pay close attention to the energy around you. But first, you must be willing, you must be open, and you must consciously *receive* the "Rays of Light."

Know that the frequencies of the "Rays of Light" are truly *received* by a human when they are accessed. These frequencies do not come from a human. They can be accessed *through* one human, to be shared with another human, situation, source, or for yourself. In other words, the frequencies come *through* a human, not from a human. Frequencies are different from energies in that frequencies come from the Divine and are completely pure. The vibrations in these frequencies are the highest of vibrations, which is how frequencies can be transformed into a type of healing.

Know that energy is not pure like the frequencies. Energy can come from a human. Energy can be intended or released from one human to another human. Energy can come from a situation or an object as everything is energy. Energy also comes from Mother Earth.

The intention of the violet filter placed below the feet of the recipient during a healing session is to filter out the impurities in the energy being received from Mother Earth. Mother Earth is continuously absorbing energies for you and not all of those energies are of the highest vibrations. Therefore, it is recommended that low vibrating energies be filtered before Mother Earth infuses them into the recipient during a session.

Notice that the word recipient is used for the person receiving the frequencies during the session. Choosing this word would be a reminder that you are giving and receiving energies and frequencies at different times. At a time that you are receiving from another person, you would be a recipient. Choosing the word recipient in this case, would be using a high vibrating emotion that supports each of you equally, the person providing the session and the person receiving in the session, with no distinction. These roles can certainly change.

Every human being has access to the "Rays of Light." You can access the rays very simply through your intentions, with the assistance of your Divine Source, the Angels, and your guides. Remember, it is all about the intention. The "Rays of Light" are not coming from you when you access them; the rays are being received by you. It is merely by your simple intention and asking for assistance that you are able to receive. Always remember to be aware of the emotion attached your intention, in order to be sure that it is one of a high vibration.

Since the receiving the "Rays of Light," is through your intention, know that you can set this intention for a situation or for a recipient lying or sitting in front of you, or if they are in another location, in another state, or in another country. Again, it is all about the intention, the asking, trusting, and believing. Experiment and you will see how it works.

You deepen your connection with the Divine in increments, over time, each time that you receive the frequencies of the "Rays of Light." Each time that you access the "Rays of Light" through your intentions, a meditation, or the simple "Prayer of Love and Protection," you are receiving the frequencies of the rays and elevating your connection to your Divine Source and "all that is, "while deepening your connection top Mother earth and the earth energies. This connection increases little by little, and as it does so, the intensity becomes greater, little by little. Over time, your connection can become quite powerful.

Linda Street has a unique gift with the "Rays of Light" that allows her to *elevate* your Divine connection with the "Rays of Light" and with Mother Earth. This elevation will provide you access to these frequencies at a much higher level of consciousness, which further deepens and elevates your connection for yourself, and in assisting others. This elevation can deepen your connection to the Earth energies, by expanding your Crown Chakra and your Root Chakra, as you work with higher frequencies. This elevation can only be offered by Linda Street at this time.

This elevation can be completed through a class titled, '"Rays of Light" - Elevate Your Divine Connection." The two and one half day class includes your elevation, discussions on this book, additional information about the "Rays of Light," and hands on practice sessions with opportunities to practice accessing the frequencies before and after your connections have been elevated, allowing you to experience and understand the difference. This will assist you in accessing these beautiful frequencies of the "Rays of Light" with confidence, a deeper connection, and at a higher elevation for the purpose of assisting others as well as assisting yourself. This class is not for everyone, while the frequencies of the "Rays of Light" are for everyone.

As you may have noticed with the meditations and the step by step sessions, anyone can access the rays and greatly benefit from the frequencies. That is why they are here. As you begin to elevate your connection, and you begin to access the frequencies of the "Rays of Light" for yourself or for others, there is a level of very intense and powerful frequencies and assistance that you are receiving that is unmatched.

The "Rays of Light" can be accessed and used for the purpose of cleansing, healing, balancing, and re-aligning your chakras, and also for further deepening and elevating your connection through the expansion of your Crown Chakra and Root Chakra. The frequencies of the "Rays of Light" can be used for special intentions. Special intentions can be included by you or by the recipient at the beginning of a session and during the session. A recipient can intend a special intention at the beginning of a session or a special intention can be used for a period of five days as detailed in Chapter 9, "A Healing Journey".

A special intention can be anything positive that you desire to create, old patterns that you wish to dissolve, or something that you wish to strengthen in yourself. A special intention can be about a person, a situation, a concern with your physical body, sending love or assistance to this planet, a special cause, or anything of a mental, physical, emotional, or of a spiritual nature.

You will find two sets of step by step instructions used for completing a full "Rays of Light" session in Chapters 11 and 12. Both sessions complete the cleansing, healing, balancing, and re-alignment of all of your primary chakras. One set of instructions is for the '"Rays of Light" Healing and Chakra Balancing Session', with instructions to add a special intention and for the purpose of additional, general, and overall healing. This session can also be used to connect with your Divine Source, the Angels, and your guides, and to dissolve unhealthy cords that you might hold attached to situations or persons.

A second set of instructions is for the '"Rays of Light" Chakra Balancing Session.' This session includes the cleansing, healing, balancing, and re-alignment of the chakras; however, it does not include the special intention, the additional healing, or the dissolving of unhealthy cords.

If your goal is to increase your connection, your awareness, and to add to your information, you are off to a good start by reading this book. If that is not your goal, you are still ahead of the game since you now have been introduced to the information. Many have been asking questions such as, "What is a chakra?" "What do you mean by energy or frequencies?" "What are the "Rays of Light"? Some readers may know nothing about these topics or of the healing modalities but are curious to learn more about them, while other readers may have some familiarity from various sources and backgrounds.

This book is sharing not only the information and answering questions about the "Rays of Light," but is also sharing the details and steps to the "Rays of Light" meditations and healing sessions. This will enable you to experience the frequencies and energies and to have a better understanding of what takes place in a meditation or healing session. You will find everything all rolled into one, and the information is for *everyone*. The intention is to assist you toward a better understanding of the frequencies of the "Rays of Light," combined with the energies of Earth, as they are both very powerful forces.

Mother Earth is alive and surrounded by the life of humans, animals, and their growth. Mother Earth is a very powerful energy and a force that is unmatched by no other (other than Divine Source, of course). You have perhaps experienced the powerful force of hurricanes in the sea or storms on the land. This energy is available for you to use for the purpose of accessing and experiencing. That is why the "Rays of Light" and the energies of Mother Earth are both channeled for the highest possible outcome, to support your intentions and your growth, your health, and your well-being. Nature is not only very beautiful but also packs a very powerful punch.

So for those that wish to have a better understanding of the frequencies, energies, or of a chakra, and have not taken any formal courses of instruction in this area or received any training, this book can provide a better understanding of the process as well as providing information and some understanding of the terms. You will be able to use the meditations and the processes to access the frequencies of the "Rays of Light." For others that have acquired your personal experiences in these areas, this book can provide another approach by offering access to new frequencies, and hopefully, introduce you to new ideas to add to your practice or for you to use to sharpen your beautiful tools.

A good place to begin in working with the "Rays of Light" is to use the meditations, frequently, every day, if possible. This will not only bring in the frequencies and energies that shift you into to a new vibration, but the experience will also assist you to become familiar with the "Rays of Light," the energies, and how they feel to you. You can begin to understand the feelings that you experience with the frequencies and the energies and you can then experiment with them. By all means, you are encouraged to have fun and to experiment. This is encouraged as you might often times tend to become so serious when working with energies and the changes that you forget about the *having fun* part. The fun and experimentation is always with a positive intention of course.

It can be helpful, but not necessary, to have some understanding of the energies or to have previous experience in working with them. Having experience can sometimes become a hindrance by creating a hesitation to look at a new approach, or a hesitation to change an old pattern for a better option. The procedures used to access the "Rays of Light" are very unique, as are the teachings that are very much a part of the "Rays of Light." Practice is your biggest asset and your biggest teacher and is one of your keys to *listening to the dark*. Your practice in accessing the frequencies and energies and in understanding and sharing the teachings are a very important piece of your growth.

If you wish to practice, it is recommended that you read these chapters over and over again until you feel that you have a good understanding of the information. Remember to practice as you are learning. No matter whom you are, what type of job you hold, or what your background is, you can always find opportunities, places, and ways to practice with energy and accessing these frequencies.

Examples of where and when to practice can be found everywhere. Practice where you work, practice with challenging situations that arise day to day, practice creating a more joyful experience or a more joyful day for yourself, practice improving a relationship, practice a better connection to *hear* the guidance, practice releasing old patterns and situations that do not feel good, practice attracting new patterns and situations that do feel good, practice when waking up in the morning or when going to bed at night. The list can go on. Practice can be as simple as reciting the "Prayer of Love and Protection" (found in the Conclusion in this book,) in the meditations in chapter 8, in the healing sessions in Chapters 11 and 12. Accessing the "Rays of Light" can be used for any time you feel you need assistance to bring in a high vibrating emotion to replace a low vibrating emotion.

So begin by *practicing*. As long as you are learning and you see a result, you are doing it right. If you are not seeing the result that you are going for, practice some more and change it up. When you stop learning and growing, you need to re-evaluate. Each step that you take and every turn that you make is to learn something new and will take you to a greater intensity. Practicing and learning can take you to a new vibration and a new experience and with a greater intensity. Your experiences will accumulate, and as they do, you can begin to teach others what you have experienced and what you have learned. You will be creating a ripple effect and having fun doing so.

You will also begin to notice that you are growing and feeling better and better each day. You will wake up without the knots in your stomach that come from worries or fears. It will be a far different experience for you than you have ever imagined. Little by little, step by step, you can replace the old heavy patterns, and those emotions that are attached to them and weighing you down, with new patterns, experiencing the emotions of joy and happiness that feel light, wonderful, and uplifting. You will look forward to each new experience rather than the opposite. You will feel more like you are in a paradise on Earth. Isn't that the way that it is supposed to be?

In working with the frequencies of the "Rays of Light," the energies of Mother Earth, and the chakras of the human body, it is important to be mindful of the impact. The instructions for cleansing, healing, balancing, and re-aligning the chakras are designed to guide you through a specific process. You can vary slightly in your approach, as you may use a slightly different way to *feel* the energy, however, be mindful of adding or deleting steps to the procedures that are outlined in chapters 11 & 12. The meditations provide cleansing, healing, balancing, and the re-alignment of your chakras on a general level, while the healing sessions provide this on a much deeper level.

The steps to "Rays of Light" sessions are different from creating a meditation. The steps that you do and do not take when working with a human chakra, as well your steps and the actions that you take during a healing session do create, and there will be a result to your actions. You must be aware to take actions that attach high vibrating emotions which are only supportive and uplifting during a session, never the opposite. You must be sure that your action will have a positive impact and not the opposite. You must follow the steps exactly the way they are outlined in the "Rays of Light" sessions.

An example would be in a adding a practice that stops the human chakra. It is important to understand that human chakras must be in motion at all times, no matter what. A human chakra <u>must never be stopped</u>. Human chakras are always in motion and meant to be in motion. They may slow down, become sluggish and dirty, or they may become damaged. In any case, a human chakra must never be stopped. Stopping a human chakra can have a severe impact on the person. The chakras can be cleaned, repaired, balanced, and re-aligned, and infused with all of the loving frequencies of the "Rays of Light", or recharged, but a human chakra must never be stopped.

It is very important in sharing your gifts, information, and energies with others, to always honor and respect their privacy. This also includes the privacy of the fact that you had a meeting with a person and/or provided guidance and information to that person. Honor and respect another's privacy just as you would honor and respect the privacy of a friend or an acquaintance that trusts you when they share private information with you. Honor and respect other's privacy as you wish your privacy to be honored and respected. Honor *all* with that same confidentiality and respect. Information about another that is shared should be shared only for the purpose of assisting that person and for a *business purpose,* and you should have the permission of that person to share their information.

When a person feels a need or desire to share confidential information of others, there is a vibration attached. What could that vibration look like? If this vibration is of pure love and positive intentions, it could be a high vibration. If that vibration is that of a low vibration, such as judgment, gossip, or worry, take a close look at the *whole picture*. Could that person be adding a judgment or worry such as, "Oh my gosh, they need help," or one of "They are surely going about this the wrong way." There is no right or wrong, only choices. Could that person be comparing themselves to another or talking about another for the purpose boosting their own confidence? Again, this would be creating a low vibration. Is that what you want to create and attract?

Choose a healthy option to boost your emotions and the emotions of others. Create a healthy ripple effect. Choose high vibrating and healthy emotions to create a positive and loving ripple effect. Remember, you are not perfect, you are human. If you catch yourself creating a low vibration, stop, look, and choose to create something different. Create what you really want to receive. Create what feels good to you and to others. And remember to *be* that light and that shining example to others as you work with the frequencies and energies. *Live it.*

Chapter Eleven
"Rays of Light" Healing and Chakra Balancing Session

Chapter Eleven: "Rays of Light" Healing and Chakra Balancing Session

"Rays of Light" Healing and Chakra Balancing Session

This chapter presents a set of instructions for the '"Rays of Light" Healing and Chakra Balancing Session.' These instructions are detailed for the purpose of cleansing, healing, balancing, and re-alignment of all of the primary chakras. It includes instructions for adding a special intention and is used for the purpose of additional, general, and overall healing. This session can also be used to connect with your Divine Source, the Angels, and your guides, and to dissolve and release unhealthy cords to situations or persons. You can use the diagram of the chakras in Chapter 3, **Figures 3A Primary Chakras, Front View and 3B Primary Chakras, Side View**, as a guide during the chakra cleansing and balancing. You can also play soft, calming, and soothing meditation music during the session if the recipient is comfortable with that.

This session will last approximately 60-90 minutes. This includes the time you spend sharing messages and information with the recipient. Each person is different in the time it may take to complete the cleansing, infusing the chakras, and receiving the messages. You will want to be sure to spend the time you need with each chakra, until you *feel* it is complete. Practice will assist you in understanding when a chakra *feels* complete. The more you practice; you will notice that over time, it will take less time to complete a session. A massage table, warm blanket, and soft meditation music is recommended for the recipient to be comfortable during the session.

First, provide the recipient with a brief summary of what to expect:

Share with the recipient that you will be setting your intentions. Also ask the recipient to set his/her intentions to include being open and deserving of receiving during this session. Ask the recipient what he/she would like to request as a special intention to be received during this session. In other words, what is the recipient's intention of receiving? The recipient may speak their intentions out loud if he/she wishes. Setting your intentions *out loud* can be very powerful since you live in a physical world. Assure the recipient that the frequencies will automatically go where they are needed and will assist with his/her intentions. Let the recipient know that you will be working with the Angels on each chakra, one at a time, first cleansing the chakra, then infusing the chakra with the frequencies of the "Rays of Light."

Know that you will be accessing the frequencies from the "Rays of Light" to cleanse, heal, balance, and re-align each chakra, and running these frequencies through the recipient at his/her feet and at his/her Crown Chakra. You will also be infusing the recipient and his/her aura with general healing frequencies of the "Rays of Light," and surrounding him/her in a cocoon filled with protective and healing energies at the end of the session.

During the session you will ask the Angels to assist in dissolving any unhealthy Etheric Cords attached to the recipient at this time. Etheric Cords can be seen as transparent tubing attached to a human being, with the other end attached to another human being or a situation. If the cords are unhealthy, they can drain your energy and bring in low vibrations that will deplete you and further attract energy that is unhealthy for you. Etheric Cords can very easily become attached by obsession or worry over a person or a situation for example.

Remind the recipient that it is important to continue to remain focused on his/her intentions, with high vibrating emotions, once he/she leaves your office. Also remind the recipient to pay close attention to the guidance that he/she will continue to receive on an ongoing basis, after the session is complete. The recipient will continue to receive the guidance ongoing, there is no time frame. Remind him/her to be sure to follow the guidance.

 Ask the recipient to lie on the massage table. Be sure to let the recipient know that you have a warm blanket available in case they become chilled during the session.

Next, begin your "Rays of Light" Healing and Chakra
Balancing Session:

1. Choose any method that you feel comfortable in
   grounding yourself. Feel free to use the method of
   visualizing roots growing from the bottom of your feet
   that is outlined in Chapter 8, the "Guidance and Healing
   Meditation."

2. Ask for protection. Ask all loving beings of the "Rays of
   Light" to surround you and the recipient with a veil of
   love and protection, in the physical and non-physical, on
   all levels and in all time and space. Ask for this veil to
   allow only the highest of vibrations, releasing all else,
   with love, grace, and gratitude. Thank all loving beings.

3. Ask the recipient to set his/her intentions as to what
   they wish to receive in this "Healing and Chakra
   Balancing Session." He/she can set his/her intentions
   privately, out loud, or in writing if he/she wishes. Setting
   your intentions *out loud* or in writing can be very
   powerful as you live in a physical world.

4. Let the recipient know that you will be setting your
   intentions in asking for assistance from your Divine
   Source, the Angels, and your guides etc., and that will
   take a few moments.

5. Ask your Divine Source, the Angels and your guides, the
   recipient's Angels and guides, your higher self, the
   recipient's higher self, Mother Earth, any other beings
   from the Divine realm that you wish, and all loving

beings of the "Rays of Light" to step in and assist in this session. Ask to receive clear guidance and clear messages and images to share with the recipient that are for his/her greatest benefit. Ask also for a clear understanding in the relaying of this information.

6. Once you feel the energy radiating in your palms, hold your palms facing down, over the Solar Plexus and the Sacral Chakras of the recipient. Hover your palms while you ask that the "Rays of Light" fill the recipient with the frequencies of all of the rays and "all that is" to begin this session.

7. Ask Archangel Michael to remove all energy from the recipient's aura that is not of a high vibration. Also ask Archangel Michael to remove all energy from your aura that is not of the highest vibration. Ask Archangel Michael to continue to remove these energies until you make this request again.

8. Ask Archangel Gabrielle to remove all energy that is released by the recipient during this session that is not of a high vibration. Also ask Archangel Gabrielle to remove all energy that is released by you during this session that is not of a high vibration. Ask Archangel Gabrielle to continue to remove these released energies until you make this request again.

9. Begin working with the chakras by cupping your hands over the recipient's <u>Heart Chakra</u>. It is recommended to always begin with the Heart Chakra, as this is the center of your chakras. Cup your hands into a circle hovering

directly over the Heart Chakra, without touching the skin or clothing of the recipient. If you are touching the recipient's skin or clothing, you may not *feel* the energy of the cleansing, but rather, you may be feeling the sensations of the recipient's skin or clothing. When you hover, you tend to feel only the energy.

10. Ask the Angels for assistance in cleansing out the Heart Chakra completely; ask for assistance in removing all energy that is not of a high vibration. Visualize what it might look like as the energy is being removed from the chakra. Pay very close attention to any messages or images that you receive during this time. This information is to be shared with the recipient after the session is complete. Also pay close attention to the *feel* of the energy as the cleansing is taking place. Learn how this energy feels to you. You will *feel* or notice the energy in different ways; it can be swirling, hot, cold, or pressure, etc. You may ask the Angels to please *let you know* (give you a sign) when the cleansing is complete. You may *feel* when the activity of the energy surrounding the chakra has stopped, which can indicate the cleansing is complete. Learn to recognize <u>your</u> signs so that when you know when the chakra is completely cleansed.

11. Once the cleansing of the Heart Chakra is complete, ask the Angels to assist in infusing the Heart Chakra with the "Rays of Light" and to completely fill this chakra with the frequencies of love, remembrance, and, "all that is,"

which are perfect for the recipient at this time. Hold your hands, palms facing down, hovering over the Heart Chakra, again without touching the skin or clothing of the recipient, and infuse the frequencies of the "Rays of Light" coming through your palms into the recipient's chakra. Use your intentions and visualize the "Rays of Light" streaming through your palms and into the chakra.

12. Pay very close attention to any messages or images that you receive during this time. This information is to be shared with the recipient once the healing session is complete. Also pay close attention to the *feel* of these frequencies while the infusing of the rays is taking place. Learn how these frequencies feel to you as they fill this chakra with *love*. You will *feel* or notice the frequencies in different ways; however, you will notice a gentle pressure pushing up on your palms, from the Heart Chakra, when the chakra is full. You do not want to overfill the chakra. You may also ask the Angels to please *let you know* when the chakra is full. Learn to recognize your signs so that you know when the chakra is full.

13. Once you notice the distinct pressure on your palms, indicating that the chakra is full, keeping your palms facing down, gently and slowly move your palms higher, stopping at intervals to notice the pressure to make sure that the pressure is also continuing upward. When you are feeling that pressure and your hands are following your movement upward, move your palms high enough

so that they are close to the level of your eyes. If it is more comfortable to stop a little lower, that is fine. Continue to extend your palms straight out in front of you, across from your eyes, turn your palms facing upwards and gently wave them across the top of the pressure coming from the chakra, at that level. This will seal the chakra and allow you to move your intentions on to the next chakra.

14. Next, cup your hands into a circle hovering directly over the recipient's Throat Chakra, without touching the skin or clothing of the recipient. If you are touching the recipient's skin or clothing, you may not *feel* the energy of the cleansing, but rather, you may be feeling the sensations of the recipient's skin or clothing. When you hover, you tend to feel only energy.

15. Ask the Angels for assistance in cleansing out the Throat Chakra completely; ask for assistance in removing all energy that is not of a high vibration. Visualize what it might look like as the energy is being removed from the chakra. Pay very close attention to any messages or images that you receive during this time. This information is to be shared with the recipient after the session is complete. Also pay close attention to the *feel* of the energy as the cleansing is taking place. Learn how this energy feels to you. You will *feel* or notice the energy in different ways; it can feel swirling, hot, cold, or pressure, etc. You may ask the Angels to please *let you*

know (give you a sign) when the cleansing is complete. You may also *feel* when the activity of the energy surrounding the chakra has stopped, letting you know that it is complete. Learn to recognize your signs so that you know when that the chakra is completely cleansed.

16. Once the cleansing of the Throat Chakra is complete, ask the Angels to assist in infusing the Throat chakra with the "Rays of Light" and to completely fill this chakra with the frequencies of love, remembrance, and "all that is," which are perfect for the recipient at this time. Hold your hands, palms facing down, hovering over the Throat Chakra, again without touching the skin or clothing of the recipient, and infuse the frequencies of the "Rays of Light" coming through your palms into the recipient's chakra. Use your intentions and visualize the "Rays of Light" streaming through your palms into the chakra.

17. Pay very close attention to any messages or images that you receive during this time. This information is to be shared with the recipient once the healing session is complete. Also pay close attention to the *feel* of these frequencies while the infusing of the "Rays of Light" is taking place. Learn how these frequencies feel to you as they fill this chakra with *love*. You will *feel* or notice the frequencies in different ways; however, you will notice a gentle pressure pushing up on your palms, from the Throat Chakra, when the chakra is full. You do not want to overfill the chakra. You may also ask the Angels to

please *let you know* when the chakra is full. Learn to recognize <u>your</u> signs so that you know when the chakra is full.

18. Once you notice the distinct pressure on your palms, indicating that the chakra is full, keeping your palms facing down, gently and slowly move your palms higher, stopping at intervals to notice the pressure to make sure that the pressure is also continuing upward. When you are feeling that pressure and your hands are following your movement upward, move your palms high enough so that they are close to the level of your eyes. If it is more comfortable to stop a little lower, that is fine. Continue to extend your palms straight out in front of you, across from your eyes, turn your palms facing upwards and gently wave them across the top of the pressure coming from the chakra, at that level. This will seal the chakra and allow you to move your intentions on to the next chakra.

19. Next, cup your hands into a circle hovering directly over the recipient's <u>Third Eye Chakra</u>, without touching the skin or clothing of the recipient. If you are touching the recipient's skin or clothing, you may not *feel* the energy of the cleansing, but rather, you may be feeling the sensations of the recipient's skin or clothing. When you hover, you tend to feel only energy.

20. Ask the Angels for assistance in cleansing out the Third Eye Chakra completely; ask for assistance in removing all

energy that is not of a high vibration. Visualize what it might look like as the energy is being removed from the chakra. Pay very close attention to any messages or images that you receive during this time. This information is to be shared with the recipient after the session is complete. Also pay close attention to the *feel* of the energy as the cleansing is taking place. Learn how this energy feels to you. You will *feel* or notice the energy in different ways; it can feel swirling, hot, cold, or pressure, etc. You may ask the Angels to please *let you know* (give you a sign) when the cleansing is complete. You may also *feel* when the activity of the energy surrounding the chakra has stopped, letting you know that it is complete. Learn to recognize your signs so that you know when that the chakra is completely cleansed.

21. Once the cleansing of the Third Eye chakra is complete, ask the Angels to assist in infusing the Third Eye Chakra with the "Rays of Light" and to completely fill this chakra with the frequencies of love, remembrance, and "all that is," which are perfect for the recipient at this time. Hold your hands, palms facing down, hovering over the Third Eye Chakra, again without touching the skin or clothing of the recipient, and infuse the frequencies of the "Rays of Light" coming through your palms into the recipient's chakra. Use your intentions and visualize the "Rays of Light" streaming through your palms into the chakra.

22. Pay very close attention to any messages or images that you receive during this time. This information is to

be shared with the recipient once the healing session is complete. Also pay close attention to the *feel* of these frequencies while the infusing of the "Rays of Light" is taking place. Learn how these frequencies feel to you as they fill this chakra with *love*. You will *feel* or notice the frequencies in different ways; however, you will notice a gentle pressure pushing up on your palms, from the Third Eye Chakra, when the chakra is full. You do not want to overfill the chakra. You may also ask the Angels to please *let you know* when the chakra is full. Learn to recognize your signs so that you know when the chakra is full.

23. Once you notice the distinct pressure on your palms, indicating that the chakra is full, keeping your palms facing down, gently and slowly move your palms higher, stopping at intervals to notice the pressure to make sure that the pressure is also continuing upward. When you are feeling that pressure and your hands are following your movement upward, move your palms high enough so that they are close to the level of your eyes. If it is more comfortable to stop a little lower, that is fine. Continue to extend your palms straight out in front of you, across from your eyes, turn your palms facing upwards and gently wave them across the top of the pressure coming from the chakra, at that level. This will seal the chakra and allow you to move your intentions on to the next chakra.

24. Next, cup your hands into a circle hovering directly over the recipient's <u>Crown Chakra</u>, without touching the skin or clothing of the recipient. If you are touching the recipient's skin or clothing, you may not *feel* the energy of the cleansing, but rather, you may be feeling the sensations of the recipient's skin or clothing. When you hover, you tend to feel only energy.

25. Ask the Angels for assistance in cleansing out the Crown Chakra completely; ask assistance in removing all energy that is not of a high vibration. Visualize what it might look like as the energy is being removed from the chakra. Pay very close attention to any messages or images that you receive during this time. This information is to be shared with the recipient after the session is complete. Also pay close attention to the *feel* of the energy as the cleansing is taking place. Learn how this energy feels to you. You will *feel* or notice the energy in different ways; it can feel swirling, hot, cold, or pressure, etc. You may ask the Angels to please *let you know* (give you a sign) when the cleansing is complete. You may also *feel* when the activity of the energy surrounding the chakra has stopped, letting you know that it is complete. Learn to recognize <u>your </u>signs so that you know when the chakra is completely cleansed.

26. Once the cleansing of the Crown Chakra is complete, ask the Angels to assist in infusing the Crown Chakra with the "Rays of Light" and to completely fill this chakra with the frequencies of love, remembrance, and "all that

is," which are perfect for the recipient at this time. Hold your hands, palms facing down, hovering over the Crown Chakra, again without touching the skin or clothing of the recipient, and infuse the frequencies of the "Rays of Light" coming through your palms into the recipient's chakra. Use your intentions and visualize the "Rays of Light" streaming through your palms into the chakra.

27. Pay very close attention to any messages or images that you receive during this time. This information is to be shared with the recipient once the healing session is complete. Also pay close attention to the *feel* of these frequencies as the infusing of the "Rays of Light" is taking place. Learn how these frequencies feel to you as they fill this chakra with *love*. You will *feel* or notice the frequencies in different ways; however, you will notice a gentle pressure pushing up on your palms, from the Crown Chakra, when the chakra is full. You do not want to overfill the chakra. You may also ask the Angels to please *let you* know when the chakra is full. Learn to recognize your signs so that you know when the chakra is full.

28. Once you notice the distinct pressure on your palms, indicating that the chakra is full, keeping your palms facing down, gently and slowly move your palms higher, stopping at intervals to notice the pressure to make sure that the pressure is also continuing upward. When you are feeling that pressure and your hands are following your movement upward, move your palms high enough

so that they are close to the level of your eyes. If it is more comfortable to stop a little lower, that is fine. Continue to extend your palms straight out in front of you, across from your eyes, turn your palms facing upwards and gently wave them across the top of the pressure coming from the chakra, at that level. This will seal the chakra and allow you to move your intentions on to the next chakra.

29. Next, hold your hands directly over the recipient's <u>Star Chakra,</u> shaping your hands around the visualization of the middle of the cone, above the recipient's Crown Chakra. Notice that this chakra is different than the other chakras. It is swirling in a cone shape above the Crown Chakra, with the swirling motion of the energy interlocking with the Stargate Chakra.

30. Ask the Angels for assistance cleansing out the Star Chakra completely; ask for assistance in removing all energy that is not of a high vibration. Visualize what it might look like as the energy is being removed from the chakra. Move your hands back and forth, in a semi-circular motion, surrounding this Star Chakra as the cleansing is taking place. This motion will assist in releasing any unwanted energy. Pay very close attention to any messages or images that you receive during this time. This information is to be shared with the recipient after the session is complete. Also pay close attention to the *feel* of the energy as the cleansing is taking place. Learn how this energy feels to you. You will *feel* or notice

the energy in different ways; it can feel swirling, hot, cold or pressure, etc. You may ask the Angels to please *let you know* (give you a sign) when the cleansing is complete. You may also *feel* when the activity of the energy surrounding the chakra has stopped, letting you know that it is complete. Learn to recognize your signs so that you know when the chakra is completely cleansed. Often times this chakra is cleansed much quicker than the time taken to cleanse the body chakras.

31. Once the cleansing of the Star Chakra is complete, ask the Angels to assist in infusing the Star Chakra with the "Rays of Light" and to completely fill this chakra with the frequencies of love, remembrance, and "all that is," which are perfect for the recipient at this time. Hold your hands, palms facing down, hovering over the Star Chakra, and infuse the frequencies of the "Rays of Light" coming through your palms into the recipient's chakra. Cup your hands on either side of the cone that you are visualizing. Use your intentions to visualize the "Rays of Light" streaming through your palms into the chakra.

32. Pay very close attention to any messages or images that you receive during this time. This information is to be shared with the recipient once the healing session is complete. Also pay close attention to the *feel* of these frequencies as the infusing of the "Rays of Light" is taking place. Learn how these frequencies feel to you as they fill this chakra with *love*. You will *feel* or notice the frequencies in different ways; however, you will notice a

gentle pressure pushing up on your palms, from the Star Chakra, when the chakra is full. You do not want to over fill the chakra. You may also ask the Angels to please *let you know* when the chakra is full. Learn to recognize your signs so that you know when the chakra is full.

33. Once you notice the distinct pressure on your palms, indicating that the chakra is full, keeping your palms facing down, gently and slowly move your palms higher, stopping at intervals to notice the pressure to make sure that the pressure is also continuing upward. When you are feeling that pressure and your hands are following your movement upward, move your palms high enough so that they are close to the level of your eyes. If it is more comfortable to stop a little lower, that is fine. Continue to extend your palms straight out in front of you, across from your eyes, turn your palms facing upwards and gently wave them across the top of the pressure coming from the chakra, at that level. This will seal the chakra and allow you to move your intentions on to the next chakra.

34. Next, hold your hands directly over the recipient's Stargate Chakra, shaping your hands around the visualization of the middle of the cone, and above the recipient's Crown Chakra. Notice that this chakra is different than the other chakras. It is swirling in a cone shape above the Crown Chakra, with the swirling motion of the energy interlocking with the Star Chakra.

35. Ask the Angels for assistance cleansing out the Stargate Chakra completely; ask for assistance in removing all energy that is not of a high vibration. Visualize what it might look like as the energy is being removed from the chakra. Move your hands back and forth, in a semi-circular motion, surrounding this Stargate Chakra as the cleansing is taking place. This motion will assist in releasing any unwanted energy. Pay very close attention to any messages or images that you receive during this time. This information is to be shared with the recipient after the session is complete. Also pay close attention to the *feel* of the energy as the cleansing is taking place. Learn how this energy feels to you. You will *feel* or notice the energy in different ways; it can feel swirling, hot, cold, or pressure, etc. You may ask the Angels to please *let you know* (give you a sign) when the cleansing is complete. You may also *feel* when the activity of the energy surrounding the chakra has stopped, letting you know that it is complete. Learn to recognize <u>your</u> signs so that you know when the chakra is completely cleansed. Often times this chakra is cleansed much quicker than the time taken to cleanse the body chakras.

36. Once the cleansing of the Stargate Chakra is complete, ask the Angels to assist in infusing the Stargate Chakra with the "Rays of Light" and to completely fill this chakra with the frequencies of love, remembrance, and "all that is," which are perfect for the recipient at this time. Hold your hands, palms facing down, hovering over the

Stargate Chakra, and infuse the frequencies of the "Rays of Light" coming from your palms into the recipient's chakra. Cup your hands on either side of the cone that you are visualizing. Use your intentions and visualize the "Rays of Light" streaming through your palms into the chakra.

37. Pay very close attention to any messages or images that you receive during this time. This information is to be shared with the recipient once the healing session is complete. Also pay close attention to the *feel* of these frequencies as the infusing of the "Rays of Light" is taking place. Learn how these frequencies feel to you as they fill this chakra with *love*. You will *feel* or notice these frequencies in different ways; however, you will notice a gentle pressure pushing up on your palms, from the Stargate Chakra, when the chakra is full. You do not want to over fill the chakra. You may also ask the Angels to please *let you know* when the chakra is full. Learn to recognize your signs so that you know when the chakra is full.

38. Once you notice the distinct pressure on your palms, indicating that the chakra is full, keeping your palms facing down, gently and slowly move your palms higher, stopping at intervals to notice the pressure to make sure that the pressure is also continuing upward. When you are feeling that pressure and your hands are following your movement upward, move your palms high enough so that they are close to the level of your eyes. If it is

more comfortable to stop a little lower, that is fine. Continue to extend your palms straight out in front of you, across from your eyes, turn your palms facing upwards and gently wave them across the top of the pressure coming from the chakra, at that level. This will seal the chakra and allow you to move your intentions on to the next chakra.

39. Next, hold your hands directly over the recipient's Supernova Chakra, shaping your hands around the visualization of the upper end of the cone, and above the recipient's Crown Chakra. Notice that this chakra is different than all of the other chakras (including the Star and the Stargate Chakras). It is swirling on the outside of the cone shape, above the Star and Stargate Chakras, weaving downwards towards the point of the cone.

40. Ask the Angels for assistance in cleansing out the Supernova Chakra completely; ask for assistance in removing all energy that is not of a high vibration. Visualize what it might look like as the energy is being removed from the chakra. Move your hands back and forth, in a semi-circular motion, surrounding this Supernova Chakra as the cleansing is taking place. This motion will assist releasing any unwanted energy. Pay very close attention to any messages or images that you receive during this time. This information is to be shared with the recipient after the session is complete. Also pay close attention to the *feel of the energy* as the cleansing is taking place. Learn how this energy feels to you.

You will *feel* or notice the energy in different ways; it can feel swirling, hot, cold, or pressure, etc. You may ask the Angels to please *let you know* (give you a sign) when the cleansing is complete. You may also *feel* when the activity of the energy surrounding the chakra has stopped, letting you know that it is complete. Learn to recognize your signs so that you know when the chakra is completely cleansed. Often times this chakra is cleansed much quicker than the time taken to cleanse the body chakras.

41. Once the cleansing of the Supernova Chakra is complete, ask the Angels to assist in infusing the Supernova Chakra with the "Rays of Light" and to completely fill this chakra with the frequencies of love, remembrance, and "all that is," which are perfect for the recipient at this time. Hold your hands, palms facing down, hovering over the Supernova Chakra, and infuse the frequencies of the "Rays of Light" coming through your palms into the recipient's chakra. Cup your hands on either side of the cone that you are visualizing. Use your intentions to visualize the "Rays of Light" streaming through your palms into the chakra.

42. Pay very close attention to any messages or images that you receive during this time. This information is to be shared with the recipient once the session is complete. Also pay close attention to the *feel* of these frequencies as the infusing of the "Rays of Light" is taking place. Learn how these frequencies feel to you as

they fill this chakra with *love*. You will *feel* or notice the frequencies in different ways; however, you will notice a gentle pressure pushing up on your palms, from the Supernova Chakra, when the chakra is full. You do not want to over fill the chakra. You may also ask the Angels to please *let you know* when the chakra is full. Learn to recognize your signs so that you know when the chakra is full.

43. Once you notice the distinct pressure on your palms, indicating that the chakra is full, keeping your palms facing down, gently and slowly move your palms higher, stopping at intervals to notice the pressure to make sure that the pressure is also continuing upward. When you are feeling that pressure and your hands are following your movement upward, move your palms high enough so that they are close to the level of your eyes. If it is more comfortable to stop a little lower, that is fine. Continue to extend your palms straight out in front of you, across from your eyes, turn your palms facing upwards and gently wave them across the top of the pressure coming from the chakra, at that level. This will seal the chakra and allow you to move your intentions on to the next chakra.

44. Hold both of your hands above the recipient's Heart Chakra; use a sweeping motion to sweep away the energies and frequencies from the Heart Chakra up past the Supernova Chakra, eight separate times. This sweeping motion is aligning the chakras.

45. Next, cup your hands into a circle hovering directly over the <u>Solar Plexus Chakra</u>, without touching the skin or clothing of the recipient. If you are touching the recipient's skin or clothing, you may not *feel* the energy of the cleansing, but rather, you may be feeling the sensations of the recipient's skin or clothing. When you hover, you tend to feel only energy.

46. Ask the Angels for assistance in cleansing out the Solar Plexus Chakra completely; ask the Angels to assist in removing all energy that is not of a high vibration. Visualize what it might look like as the energy is being removed from the chakra. Pay very close attention to any messages or images that you receive during this time. This information is to be shared with the recipient after the session is complete. Also pay close attention to the *feel* of the energy as the cleansing is taking place. Learn how this energy feels to you. You will *feel* or notice the energy in different ways; it can be swirling, hot, cold or pressure, etc. You may ask the Angels to please *let you know* (give you a sign) when the cleansing is complete. You may also *feel* when the activity of the energy surrounding the chakra has stopped, letting you know it is complete. Learn to recognize <u>your</u> signs so that you know when the chakra is completely cleansed.

47. Once the cleansing of the Solar Plexus Chakra is complete, ask the Angels to assist in infusing the Solar Plexus Chakra with the "Rays of Light" and to completely fill this chakra with the frequencies of love,

remembrance, and "all that is," which are perfect for the recipient at this time. Hold your hands, palms facing down, hovering over the Solar Plexus Chakra, again without touching the skin or clothing of the recipient, and infuse the frequencies of the "Rays of Light" that are coming through your palms into the recipient's chakra. Use your intentions and visualize the "Rays of Light" streaming through your palms into the chakra.

48. Pay very close attention to any messages or images that you receive during this time. This information is to be shared with the recipient once the session is complete. Also pay close attention to the *feel* of these frequencies as the infusing of the "Rays of Light" is taking place. Learn how these frequencies feel to you as they fill this chakra with *love*. You will *feel* or notice the frequencies in different ways; however, you will notice a gentle pressure pushing up on your palms, from the Solar Plexus Chakra, when the chakra is full. You do not want to overfill the chakra. You may also ask the Angels to please *let you know* when the chakra is full. Learn to recognize your signs so that you know when the chakra is full.

49. Once you notice the distinct pressure on your palms, indicating that the chakra is full, keeping your palms facing down, gently and slowly move your palms higher, stopping at intervals to notice the pressure to make sure that the pressure is also continuing upward. When you are feeling that pressure and your hands are following

your movement upward, move your palms high enough so that they are close to the level of your eyes. If it is more comfortable to stop a little lower, that is fine. Continue to extend your palms straight out in front of you, across from your eyes, turn your palms facing upwards and gently wave them across the top of the pressure coming from the chakra, at that level. This will seal the chakra and allow you to move your intentions on to the next chakra.

50. Next, cup your hands into a circle hovering directly over the <u>Sacral Chakra</u>, without touching the skin or clothing of the recipient. If you are touching the recipient's skin or clothing, you may not *feel* the energy of the cleansing, but rather, you may be feeling the sensations of the recipient's skin or clothing. When you hover, you tend to feel only energy.

51. Ask the Angels for assistance in cleansing out the Sacral Chakra completely; ask the Angels to assist in removing all energy that is not of a high vibration. Visualize what it might look like as the energy is being removed from the chakra. Pay very close attention to any messages or images that you receive during this time. This information is to be shared with the recipient after the session is complete. Also pay close attention to the *feel* of the energy as the cleansing is taking place. Learn how this energy feels to you. You will *feel* or notice the energy in different ways; it can be swirling, hot, cold, or pressure, etc. You may ask the Angels to please *let you*

know (give you a sign) when the cleansing is complete. You may also *feel* when the activity of the energy surrounding the chakra has stopped, letting you know it is complete. Learn to recognize your signs so that you know when the chakra is completely cleansed.

52. Once the cleansing of the Sacral Chakra is complete, ask the Angels to assist in infusing the Sacral Chakra with the "Rays of Light" and to completely fill this chakra with the frequencies of love, remembrance, and "all that is," which are perfect for the recipient at this time. Hold your hands, palms facing down, hovering over the Sacral Chakra, again without touching the skin or clothing of the recipient, and infuse the frequencies of the "Rays of Light" that are coming through your palms into the recipient's chakra. Use your intentions and visualize the "Rays of Light" streaming through your palms into the chakra.

53. Pay very close attention to any messages or images that you receive during this time. This information is to be shared with the recipient once the session is complete. Also pay close attention to the *feel* of these frequencies as the infusing of the "Rays of Light" is taking place. Learn how these frequencies feel to you as they fill this chakra with *love*. You will *feel* or notice the frequencies in different ways; however, you will notice a gentle pressure pushing up on your palms, from the Sacral Chakra, when the chakra is full. You do not want to overfill the chakra. You may also ask the Angels to

please *let you know* when the chakra is full. Learn to recognize your signs so that you know when the chakra is full.

54. Once you notice the distinct pressure on your palms, indicating that the chakra is full, keeping your palms facing down, gently and slowly move your palms higher, stopping at intervals to notice the pressure to make sure that the pressure is also continuing upward. When you are feeling that pressure and your hands are following your movement upward, move your palms high enough so that they are close to the level of your eyes. If it is more comfortable to stop a little lower that is fine. Continue to extend your palms straight out in front of you, across from your eyes, turn your palms facing upwards and gently wave them across the top of the pressure coming from the chakra, at that level. This will seal the chakra and allow you to move your intentions on to the next chakra.

55. Next, cup your hands into a circle hovering directly over the Base Chakra, without touching the skin or clothing of the recipient. If you are touching the recipient's skin or clothing, you may not *feel* the energy of the cleansing, but rather, you may be feeling the sensations of the recipient's skin or clothing. When you hover, you tend to feel only energy.

56. Ask the Angels for assistance in cleansing out the Base Chakra completely; ask the Angels for assistance in removing all energy that is not of a high vibration.

Visualize what it might look like as the energy is being removed from the chakra. Pay very close attention to any messages or images that you receive during this time. This information is to be shared with the recipient after the session is complete. Also pay close attention to the *feel* of the energy as the cleansing is taking place. Learn how this energy feels to you. You will *feel* or notice the energy in different ways; it can be swirling, hot, cold or pressure, etc. You may ask the Angels to please *let you know* (give you a sign) when the cleansing is complete. You may also *feel* when the activity of the energy surrounding the chakra has stopped, letting you know that it is complete. Learn to recognize your signs so that you know when the chakra is completely cleansed.

57. Once the cleansing of the Base Chakra is complete, ask the Angels to assist in infusing the Base Chakra with the "Rays of Light" and to completely fill this chakra with the frequencies of love, remembrance, and "all that is," which are perfect for the recipient at this time. Hold your hands, palms facing down, hovering over the Base Chakra, again without touching the skin or clothing of the recipient, and infuse the frequencies of the "Rays of Light" that are coming through your palms into the recipient's chakra. Use your intentions and visualize the "Rays of Light" streaming through your palms into the chakra.

58. Pay very close attention to any messages or images that you receive during this time. This information is to be shared with the recipient once the session is complete. Also pay close attention to the *feel* of these frequencies as the infusing of the "Rays of Light" is taking place. Learn how these frequencies feel to you as they fill this chakra with *love*. You will *feel* or notice the frequencies in different ways; however, you will notice a gentle pressure pushing up on your palms, from the Base Chakra, when the chakra is full. You do not want to over fill the chakra. You may also ask the Angels to please *let you know* when the chakra is full. Learn to recognize your signs so that you know when the chakra is full.

59. Once you notice the distinct pressure on your palms, indicating that the chakra is full, keeping your palms facing down, gently and slowly move your palms higher, stopping at intervals to notice the pressure to make sure that the pressure is also continuing upward. When you are feeling that pressure and your hands are following your movement upward, move your palms high enough so that they are close to the level of your eyes. If it is more comfortable to stop a little lower, that is fine. Continue to extend your palms straight out in front of you, across from your eyes, turn your palms facing upwards and gently wave them across the top of the pressure coming from the chakra, at that level. This will seal the chakra and allow you to move your intentions on to the next chakra.

60. Next, cup your hands into a circle hovering directly over the <u>Root Chakra</u>, without touching the skin or clothing of the recipient. If you are touching the recipient's skin or clothing, you may not *feel* the energy of the cleansing, but rather, you may be feeling the sensations of the recipient's skin or clothing. When you hover, you tend to feel only energy.

61. Ask the Angles for assistance in cleansing out the Root Chakra completely; ask the Angels for assistance in removing all energy that is not of a high vibration. Visualize what it might look like as the energy is being removed from the chakra. Pay very close attention to any messages or images that you receive during this time. This information is to be shared with the recipient after the session is complete. Also pay close attention to the *feel* of the energy as the cleansing is taking place. Learn how this energy feels to you. You will *feel* or notice the energy in different ways; it can be swirling, hot, cold or pressure, etc. You may ask the Angels to please *let you know* (give you a sign) when the cleansing is complete. You may also *feel* when the activity of the energy surrounding the chakra has stopped, letting you know that it is complete. Learn to recognize <u>your</u> signs so that you know when the chakra is completely cleansed.

62. Once the cleansing of the Root Chakra is complete, ask the Angels to assist in infusing the Root Chakra with the "Rays of Light" and to completely fill this chakra with the

frequencies of love, remembrance, and "all that is," which are perfect for the recipient at this time. Hold your hands, palms facing down, hovering over the Root Chakra, again without touching the skin or clothing of the recipient, and infuse the frequencies of the "Rays of Light" that are coming through your palms into the recipient's chakra. Use your intentions and visualize the "Rays of Light" streaming through your palms into the chakra.

63. Pay very close attention to any messages or images that you receive during this time. This information is to be shared with the recipient once the session is complete. Also pay close attention to the *feel* of these frequencies as the infusing of the "Rays of Light" is taking place. Learn how these frequencies feel to you as they fill this chakra with *love*. You will *feel* or notice the frequencies in different ways; however, you will notice a gentle pressure pushing up on your palms, from the Root Chakra, when the chakra is full. You do not want to over fill the chakra. You may also ask the Angels to please *let you know* when the chakra is full. Learn to recognize your signs so that you know when the chakra is full.

64. Once you notice the distinct pressure on your palms, indicating that the chakra is full, keeping your palms facing down, gently and slowly move your palms higher, stopping at intervals to notice the pressure to make sure that the pressure is also continuing upward. When you are feeling that pressure and your hands are following

your movement upward, move your palms high enough so that they are close to the level of your eyes. If it is more comfortable to stop a little lower that is fine. Continue to extend your palms straight out in front of you, across from your eyes, turn your palms facing upwards and gently wave them across the top of the pressure coming from the chakra, at that level. This will seal the chakra and allow you to move your intentions on to the next chakra.

65. Next, cup your hands into a circle hovering directly over the Earth Star Chakra.

66. Ask the Angels for assistance in cleansing out the Earth Star Chakra completely; ask the Angels for assistance in removing all energy that is not of a high vibration. Move your hands back and forth, in a circular motion (as if you are rubbing the outside of a ball), surrounding this Earth Star Chakra as the cleansing is taking place. This motion will assist in releasing any unwanted energy. Visualize what it might look like as the energy is being removed from the chakra. Pay very close attention to any messages or images that you receive during this time. This information is to be shared with the recipient after the session is complete. Also pay close attention to the feel of the energy as the cleansing is taking place. Learn how this energy feels to you. You will feel or notice the energy in different ways; it can be swirling, hot, cold, or pressure, etc. You may ask the Angels to please let you know (give you a sign) when the cleansing is complete.

You may also *feel* when the activity of the energy surrounding the chakra has stopped, letting you know it is complete. Learn to recognize <u>your</u> signs for when you know that the chakra is completely cleansed.

67. Once the cleansing of the Earth Star Chakra is complete, ask the Angels to assist in infusing the Earth Star Chakra with the "Rays of Light" and to completely fill this chakra with the frequencies of love, remembrance, and "all that is," which are perfect for the recipient at this time. Hold your hands, palms facing down, hovering over the Earth Star Chakra, and infuse the frequencies of the "Rays of Light" that are coming through your palms into the recipient's chakra. Use your intentions and visualize the "Rays of Light" streaming through your palms into the chakra.

68. Pay very close attention to any messages or images that you receive during this time. This information is to be shared with the recipient once the session is complete. Also pay close attention to the *feel* of these frequencies as the infusing of the "Rays of Light" is taking place. Learn how these frequencies feel to you as they fill this chakra with *love*. You will *feel* or notice the frequencies in different ways; however, you will notice a gentle pressure pushing up on your palms, from the Earth Star Chakra, when the chakra is full. You do not want to overfill the chakra. You may also ask the Angels to please *let you know* when the chakra is full. Learn to

recognize <u>your</u> signs so that you know when the chakra is full.

69. Once you notice the distinct pressure on your palms, indicating that the chakra is full, keeping your palms facing down, gently and slowly move your palms higher, stopping at intervals to notice the pressure to make sure that the pressure is also continuing upward. When you are feeling that pressure and your hands are following your movement upward, move your palms high enough so that they are close to the level of your eyes. If it is more comfortable to stop a little lower that is fine. Continue to extend your palms straight out in front of you, across from your eyes, turn your palms facing upwards and gently wave them across the top of the pressure coming from the chakra, at that level. This will seal the chakra and allow you to move your intentions on to the next chakra.

70. Next, cup your hands into a circle hovering directly over the <u>Earth Heart Chakra</u>.

71. Ask the Angels for assistance in cleansing out the Earth Heart Chakra completely; ask the Angels for assistance in removing all energy that is not of a high vibration. Move your hands back and forth, in a circular motion (as if you are rubbing the outside of a ball), surrounding this Earth Heart Chakra as the cleansing is taking place. This motion will assist in releasing any unwanted energy. Visualize what it might look like as the energy is being removed from the chakra. Pay very close attention to

any messages or images that you receive during this time. This information is to be shared with the recipient after the session is complete. Also pay close attention to the *feel* of the energy as the cleansing is taking place. Learn how this energy feels to you. You will *feel* or notice the energy in different ways; it can be swirling, hot, cold, or pressure, etc. You may ask the Angels to please *let you know* (give you a sign) when the cleansing is complete. You may also *feel* when the activity of the energy surrounding the chakra has stopped, letting you know it is complete. Learn to recognize your signs so that you know when the chakra is completely cleansed.

72. Once the cleansing of the Earth Heart Chakra is complete, ask the Angels to assist in infusing the Earth Heart Chakra with the "Rays of Light" and to completely fill this chakra with the frequencies of love, remembrance, and "all that is," which are perfect for the recipient at this time. Hold your hands, palms facing down, hovering over the Earth Heart Chakra, and infuse the frequencies of the "Rays of Light" that are coming through your palms into the recipient's chakra. Use your intentions and visualize the "Rays of Light" streaming through your palms into the chakra.

73. Pay very close attention to any messages or images that you receive during this time (This information is to be shared with the recipient once the session is complete.) Also pay close attention to the *feel* of these frequencies as the infusing of the "Rays of Light" is

taking place. Learn how these frequencies feel to you as they fill this chakra with *love*. You will *feel* or notice the frequencies in different ways; however, you will notice a gentle pressure pushing up on your palm, from the Earth Star Chakra, when the chakra is full. You do not want to overfill the chakra. You may also ask the Angels to please *let you know* when the chakra is full. Learn to recognize <u>your</u> signs so that you know when the chakra is full.

74. Once you notice the distinct pressure on your palms, indicating that the chakra is full, keeping your palms facing down, gently and slowly move your palms higher, stopping at intervals to notice the pressure to make sure that the pressure is also continuing upward. When you are feeling that pressure and your hands are following your movement upward, move your palms high enough so that they are close to the level of your eyes. If it is more comfortable to stop a little lower, that is fine. Continue to extend your palms straight out in front of you, across from your eyes, turn your palms facing upwards and gently wave them across the top of the pressure coming from the chakra, at that level. This will seal the chakra and allow you to move your intentions on to the next chakra.

75. Hold both of your hands above the recipient's Heart Chakra; use a sweeping motion to sweep away the energies and frequencies from the Heart Chakra down past the Earth Heart Chakra, eight separate times. This sweeping motion is aligning the chakras.

76. Ask Archangel Michael (or any Angel of your choosing) to remove and dissolve any unhealthy cords that may be attached to the recipient. Ask for them to be dissolved with gentleness and with love, sending love to the other person or event and to the recipient. Ask Archangel Michael to heal the areas of the recipient's body that were affected by the dissolved cords, in the physical and non-physical, on all levels and in all time and space. Give gratitude for the lessons that occurred from any cords that were dissolved.

77. Step to the feet of the recipient, facing your open palms toward the bottoms of their feet. Ask for the frequencies of the "Rays of Light" to fill the recipient's entire body, cleansing, healing, balancing, and re-aligning all of their chakras, every cell in their body and their aura, in the physical and non-physical, on all levels and in all time and space. Stay in this position for a minute or two until you feel that this is complete.

78. Step to the head of the recipient, facing your open palms toward their Crown Chakra. Ask the ask for the frequencies of the "Rays of Light" to fill the recipient's entire body, cleansing, healing, balancing, and re-aligning all of their chakras, every cell in their body and their aura, in the physical and non-physical, on all levels and in all time and space. Stay in this position for a minute or two until you feel that this is complete.

79. Step to the side of the recipient, stretching your arms to both sides of your body, with your palms stretched

out and one palm facing the recipient's Supernova Chakra above their Crown Chakra, and the other palm facing the recipient's Earth Heart Chakra below their feet. Ask for the frequencies of the "Rays of Light" to continue to infuse the recipient's entire body, cleansing, healing, balancing, and re-aligning all of their chakras, in the physical and non-physical, on all levels and in all time and space. Ask for the recipient to be filled with love, grace, gratitude, and remembrance of "all that is." Ask for the frequencies of "Rays of Light" to continue to infuse all of the recipient's chakras, every cell in their body and their entire aura with unconditional love, bringing them into harmony and balance with love and remembrance, light and darkness, and "all that is." Stay in this position for a moment or two until you feel that this is complete. Hold your arms out about eye level, with your palms face down over the recipient, until you *feel* the pressure of the frequencies and energies has reached the height of your palms.

80. Once you feel the completion, place your palms at the bottom of the recipient's feet. Sweep your palms over the recipient to the top of their Crown Chakra, surrounding them in what might be visualized as a cocoon filled with protection and healing frequencies and energies. The session is complete.

81. Give gratitude to your Divine Source, the Angels (especially Archangel Michael and Archangel Gabrielle,) your guides, the recipient's Angels and guides, your

higher self and the recipient's higher self, Mother Earth, any other being from the Divine realm that assisted, and all loving beings of the "Rays of Light" who have assisted you in this session.

82. Ask how the recipient feels, allowing them to slowly sit up when they are feeling grounded. Provide water for them, if they wish to assist in their grounding. Water can assist if the recipient feels light headed or disoriented. When they are comfortable enough, you can both sit back into your chairs so that you can hear about the recipient's experience and you can share the messages and information with the recipient that you received during the session.

83. Discuss the recipient's intentions again and assist the recipient in creating and writing positive affirmations to support their intentions. They can focus on anything they wish to create with their affirmations. Writing them on index cards allows a person to quickly and easily access the affirmations whenever and wherever they wish. This is key to promoting and using action steps to create change and growth. It is important that the recipient be aware of this. Also remind the recipient to be very mindful of their vibrations attached to their emotions in their creations. Explain to them *how it works* as you now know yourself from reading this information.

Chapter Twelve
"Rays of Light" Chakra Balancing Session

Chapter Twelve: "Rays of Light" Chakra Balancing Session

"Rays of Light" Chakra Balancing Session

This chapter presents a set of instructions for the '"Rays of Light" Chakra Balancing Session.' These instructions are detailed for the purpose of cleansing, healing, balancing, and re-alignment of all of the primary chakras. This can be used when the recipient has already experienced a full healing session or for a tune-up so to speak. You can use the diagram of the chakras in Chapter 3, **Figures 3A Primary Chakras, Front View and 3B Primary Chakras, Side View**, as a guide during the chakra cleansing and balancing. You can also play soft, calming, and soothing meditation music during the session if the recipient is comfortable with that.

This session will last approximately 45 minutes. This includes the time you spend sharing messages with the recipient. Each person is different in the time it may take to complete the cleansing, infusing the chakras, and in receiving the messages. You will want to be sure to spend the time you need with each chakra, until you *feel* it is complete. Practice will assist you in understanding when a chakra *feel*s complete. The more you practice; you will notice that over time, it will take less time to complete a session. A massage table, warm blanket, and soft meditation music is recommended for the recipient to be comfortable during the session.

First, provide the recipient a brief summary of what to expect:

Share with the recipient that you will be setting your intentions. Also ask the recipient to set his/her intentions to include being open and deserving of receiving during this session. The recipient may speak his/her intentions out loud if he/she wishes. Assure the recipient, the frequencies will automatically go where they are needed. Let the recipient know that you will be working with the Angels on each chakra, one at a time, first cleansing the chakra, then infusing the chakra with the frequencies of the "Rays of Light."

Know that you will be using the frequencies of the "Rays of Light" to cleanse, heal, balance, and re-align each chakra, and running these frequencies through the recipient at his/her feet and at his/her Crown Chakra. You will also be surrounding the recipient in a cocoon filled with protective energies at the end of the session.

Remind the recipient that it is important to continue to remain focused on his/her intentions, with high vibrating emotions, once he/she leaves your office. Also remind the recipient to pay close attention to the guidance that he/she will continue to receive on an ongoing basis, after the session is complete. The recipient will continue to receive the guidance ongoing, there is no time frame. Remind him/her to be sure to follow the guidance.

Ask the recipient to lie on the massage table. Be sure to let the recipient know that you have a warm blanket available in case they become chilled during the session.

Next, begin your "Rays of Light" Chakra Balancing Session:

1. Choose any method that you feel comfortable in grounding yourself. Feel free to use the method visualizing roots growing from the bottom of your feet that is outlined in Chapter 8, "Guidance and Healing Meditation."

2. Ask for protection. Ask all loving beings of the "Rays of Light" to surround you and the recipient with a veil of love and protection, in the physical and non-physical, on all levels and in all time and space. Ask for this veil to allow only the highest of vibrations, releasing all else, with love, grace, and gratitude. Thank all loving beings.

3. Let the recipient know that you will be setting your intentions in asking for assistance from your Divine Source, the Angels, and your guides etc., and that will take a few moments.

4. Ask your Divine Source, the Angels and your guides, the recipient's Angels and guides, your higher self, the recipient's higher self, Mother Earth, any other beings from the Divine realm that you wish, and all loving beings of the "Rays of Light" to step in and assist in this session. Ask to receive clear guidance and clear messages and images to share with the recipient that are for his/her greatest benefit. Ask also for a clear

understanding in the relaying of this information.

5. Once you feel the energy radiating in your palms, hold your palms facing down, over the Solar Plexus and the Sacral Chakras of the recipient. Hover your palms while you ask that the "Rays of Light" fill the recipient with the frequencies of all of the rays and "all that is" to begin this healing session.

6. Ask Archangel Michael to remove all energy from the recipient's aura that is not of a high vibration. Also ask Archangel Michael to remove all energy from your aura that is not of a high vibration. Ask Archangel Michael to continue to remove these energies until you make this request again.

7. Ask Archangel Gabrielle to remove all energy that is released by the recipient during this session that is not of the highest vibration. Also ask Archangel Gabrielle to remove all energy that is released by you during this session that is not of a high vibration. Ask Archangel Gabrielle to continue to remove these released energies until you make this request again.

8. Begin working with the chakras by cupping your hands over the recipient's Heart Chakra. It is recommended to always begin with the Heart Chakra, as this is the center all the chakras. Cup your hands into a circle hovering directly over the Heart Chakra, without touching the skin or clothing of the recipient. If you are touching the recipient's skin or clothing, you may not *feel* the energy

of the cleansing, but rather, you may be feeling the sensations of the recipient's skin or clothing. When you hover, you tend to feel only the energy.

9. Ask the Angels for assistance in cleansing out the Heart Chakra completely; ask for assistance in removing all energy that is not of a high vibration. Visualize what it might look like as the energy is being removed from the chakra. Pay very close attention to any messages or images that you receive during this time. This information is to be shared with the recipient after the session is complete. Also pay close attention to the *feel* of the energy as the cleansing is taking place. Learn how this energy feels to you. You will *feel* or notice the energy in different ways; it can feel swirling, hot, cold, or pressure, etc. You may ask the Angels to please *let you know* (give you a sign) when the cleansing is complete. You may *feel* when the activity of the energy surrounding the chakra has stopped, which can indicate the cleansing is complete. Learn to recognize <u>your</u> signs so that you know when the chakra is completely cleansed.

10. Once the cleansing of the Heart Chakra is complete, ask the Angels to assist in infusing the Heart Chakra with the "Rays of Light" and to completely fill this chakra with the frequencies of love, remembrance, and "all that is," which are perfect for the recipient at this time. Hold your hands, palms facing down, hovering over the Heart Chakra, again without touching the skin or clothing of

the recipient, and infuse the frequencies of the "Rays of Light" coming through your palms into the recipient's chakra. Use your intentions and visualize the "Rays of Light" streaming through your palms and into the chakra.

11. Pay very close attention to any messages or images that you receive during this time. This information is to be shared with the recipient once the session is complete. Also pay close attention to the *feel* of these frequencies as the infusing of the "Rays of Light" is taking place. Learn how these frequencies feel to you as they fill this chakra with *love*. You will *feel* or notice the frequencies in different ways; however, you will notice a gentle pressure pushing up on your palms, from the Heart Chakra, when the chakra is full. You do not want to overfill the chakra. You may also ask the Angels to please *let you know* when the chakra is full. Learn to recognize your signs so that you know when the chakra is full.

12. Once you notice the distinct pressure on your palms indicating that the chakra is full, keeping your palms facing down, gently and slowly move your palms higher, stopping at intervals to notice the pressure to make sure that the pressure is also continuing upward. When you are feeling that pressure and your hands are following your movement upward, move your palms high enough so that they are close to the level of your eyes. If it is more comfortable to stop a little lower, that is fine.

Continue to extend your palms straight out in front of you, across from your eyes, turn your palms facing upward and gently wave them across the top of the pressure coming from the chakra, at that level. This will seal the chakra and allow you to move your intentions on to the next chakra.

13. Next, cup your hands into a circle hovering directly over the recipient's <u>Throat Chakra</u>, without touching the skin or clothing of the recipient. If you are touching the recipient's skin or clothing, you may not *feel* the energy of the cleansing, but rather, you may be feeling the sensations of the recipient's skin or clothing. When you hover, you tend to feel only energy.

14. Ask the Angels for assistance in cleansing out the Throat Chakra completely; ask for assistance in removing all energy that is not of a high vibration. Visualize what it might look like as the energy is being removed from the chakra. Pay very close attention to any messages or images that you receive during this time. This information is to be shared with the recipient after the session is complete. Also pay close attention to the *feel* of the energy as the cleansing is taking place. Learn how this energy feels to you. You will *feel* or notice the energy in different ways; it can be swirling, hot, cold, or pressure, etc. You may ask the Angels to please *let you know* (give you a sign) when the cleansing is complete. You may also *feel* when the activity of the energy surrounding the chakra has stopped, letting you know

that it is complete. Learn to recognize <u>your</u> signs so that you know when the chakra is completely cleansed.

15. Once the cleansing of the Throat Chakra is complete, ask the Angels to assist in infusing the Throat Chakra with the "Rays of Light" and to completely fill this chakra with the frequencies of love, remembrance, and "all that is," which are perfect for the recipient at this time. Hold your hands, palms facing down, hovering over the Throat Chakra, again without touching the skin or clothing of the recipient, and infuse the frequencies of the "Rays of Light" coming through your palms into the recipient's chakra. Use your intentions and visualize the "Rays of Light" streaming through your palms into the chakra.

16. Pay very close attention to any messages or images that you receive during this time. This information is to be shared with the recipient once the healing session is complete. Also pay close attention to the *feel* of these frequencies as the infusing of the "Rays of Light" is taking place. Learn how these frequencies feel to you as they fill this chakra with *love*. You will *feel* or notice the frequencies in different ways; however, you will notice a gentle pressure pushing up on your palms, from the Throat Chakra, when the chakra is full. You do not want to overfill the chakra. You may also ask the Angels to please *let you know* when the chakra is full. Learn to recognize <u>your</u> signs so that you know when the chakra is full.

17. Once you notice the distinct pressure on your palms indicating that the chakra is full, keeping your palms facing down, gently and slowly move your palms higher, stopping at intervals to notice the pressure to make sure that the pressure is also continuing upward. When you are feeling that pressure and your hands are following your movement upward, move your palms high enough so that they are close to the level of your eyes. If it is more comfortable to stop a little lower, that is fine. Continue to extend your palms straight out in front of you, across from your eyes, turn your palms facing upward and gently wave them across the top of the pressure coming from the chakra, at that level. This will seal the chakra and allow you to move your intentions on to the next chakra.

18. Next, cup your hands into a circle hovering directly over the recipient's Third Eye Chakra, without touching the skin or clothing of the recipient. If you are touching the recipient's skin or clothing, you may not *feel* the energy of the cleansing, but rather, you may be feeling the sensations of the recipient's skin or clothing. When you hover, you tend to feel only energy.

19. Ask the Angels for assistance in cleansing out the Third Eye Chakra completely; ask for assistance in removing all energy that is not of a high vibration. Visualize what it might look like as the energy is being removed from the chakra. Pay very close attention to any messages or images that you receive during this time. This

.

information is to be shared with the recipient after the session is complete. Also pay close attention to the *feel* of the energy as the cleansing is taking place. Learn how this energy feels to you. You will *feel* or notice the energy in different ways; it can be swirling, hot, cold, or pressure, etc. You may ask the Angels to please *let you know* (give you a sign) when the cleansing is complete. You may also *feel* when the activity of the energy surrounding the chakra has stopped, letting you know that it is complete. Learn to recognize your signs so that you know when the chakra is completely cleansed.

20. Once the cleansing of the Third Eye Chakra is complete, ask the Angels to assist in infusing the Third Eye Chakra with the "Rays of Light" and to completely fill this chakra with the frequencies of love, remembrance, and "all that is," which are perfect for the recipient at this time. Hold your hands, palms facing down, hovering over the Third Eye Chakra, again without touching the skin or clothing of the recipient, and infuse the frequencies of the "Rays of Light" coming through your palms into the recipient's chakra. Use your intentions and visualize the "Rays of Light" streaming through your palms into the chakra.

21. Pay very close attention to any messages or images that you receive during this time. This information is to be shared with the recipient once the session is complete. Also pay close attention to the *feel* of these frequencies as the infusing of the "Rays of Light" is taking place. Learn how these frequencies feel to you as

they fill this chakra with *love*. You will *feel* or notice the frequencies in different ways; however, you will notice a gentle pressure pushing up on your palms, from the Third Eye Chakra, when the chakra is full. You do not want to overfill the chakra. You may also ask the Angels to please *let you know* when the chakra is full. Learn to recognize your signs so that you know when the chakra is full.

22. Once you notice the distinct pressure on your palms, indicating that the chakra is full, keeping your palms facing down, gently and slowly move your palms higher, stopping at intervals to notice the pressure to make sure that the pressure is also continuing upward. When you are feeling that pressure and your hands are following your movement upward, move your palms high enough so that they are close to the level of your eyes. If it is more comfortable to stop a little lower, that is fine. Continue to extend your palms straight out in front of you, across from your eyes, turn your palms facing upward and gently wave them across the top of the pressure coming from the chakra, at that level. This will seal the chakra and allow you to move your intentions on to the next chakra.

23. Next, cup your hands into a circle hovering directly over the recipient's Crown Chakra, without touching the skin or clothing of the recipient. If you are touching the recipient's skin or clothing, you may not *feel* the energy of the cleansing, but rather, you may be feeling the

sensations of the recipient's skin or clothing. When you hover, you tend to feel only energy.

24. Ask the Angels for assistance in cleansing out the Crown Chakra completely; ask for assistance in removing all energy that is not of a high vibration. Visualize what it might look like as the energy is being removed from the chakra. Pay very close attention to any messages or images that you receive during this time. This information is to be shared with the recipient after the session is complete. Also pay close attention to the *feel* of the energy as the cleansing is taking place. Learn how this energy feels to you. You will *feel* or notice the energy in different ways; it can be swirling, hot, cold, or pressure, etc. You may ask the Angels to please *let you know* (give you a sign) when the cleansing is complete. You may also *feel* when the activity of the energy surrounding the chakra has stopped, letting you know that it is complete. Learn to recognize your signs so that you know when that the chakra is completely cleansed.

25. Once the cleansing of the Crown Chakra is complete, ask the Angels to assist in infusing the Crown Chakra with the "Rays of Light" and to completely fill this chakra with the frequencies of love, remembrance, and "all that is," which are perfect for the recipient at this time. Hold your hands, palms facing down, hovering over the Crown Chakra, again without touching the skin or clothing of the recipient, and infuse the frequencies of the "Rays of Light" coming through your palms into the recipient's

chakra. Use your intentions and visualize the "Rays of Light" streaming through your palms into the chakra.

26. Pay very close attention to any messages or images that you receive during this time. This information is to be shared with the recipient once the session is complete. Also pay close attention to the *feel* of these frequencies as the infusing of the "Rays of Light" is taking place. Learn how these frequencies feel to you as they fill this chakra with *love*. You will *feel* or notice the frequencies in different ways; however, you will notice a gentle pressure pushing up on your palms, from the Crown Chakra, when the chakra is full. You do not want to overfill the chakra. You may also ask the Angels to please *let you know* when the chakra is full. Learn to recognize your signs so that you know when the chakra is full.

27. Once you notice the distinct pressure on your palms indicating that the chakra is full, keeping your palms facing down, gently and slowly move your palms higher, stopping at intervals to notice the pressure to make sure that the pressure is also continuing upward. When you are feeling that pressure and your hands are following your movement upward, move your palms high enough so that they are close to the level of your eyes. If it is more comfortable to stop a little lower, that is fine. Continue to extend your palms straight out in front of you, across from your eyes, turn your palms facing upward and gently wave them across the top of the

pressure coming from the chakra, at that level. This will seal the chakra and allow you to move your intentions on to the next chakra.

28. Next, hold your hands directly over the recipient's <u>Star Chakra</u>, shaping your hands around the visualization of the middle of a cone. Notice that this chakra is different than the other chakras. It is swirling in a cone shape above the Crown Chakra, with the swirling motion of the energy interlocking with the <u>Stargate Chakra</u>. The cone is facing upward and away from the Crown Chakra.

29. Ask the Angels for assistance cleansing out the Star Chakra completely; ask for assistance in removing all energy that is not of a high vibration. Visualize what it might look like as the energy is being removed from the chakra. Move your hands back and forth, in a semi-circular motion, surrounding this Star Chakra as the cleansing is taking place. This motion will assist in releasing any unwanted energy. Pay very close attention to any messages or images that you receive during this time. This information is to be shared with the recipient after the session is complete. Also pay close attention to the *feel* of the energy as the cleansing is taking place. Learn how this energy feels to you. You will *feel* or notice the energy in different ways; it can be swirling, hot, cold, or pressure, etc. You may ask the Angels to please *let you know* (give you a sign) when the cleansing is complete. You may also *feel* when the activity of the energy surrounding the chakra has stopped, letting you

know that it is complete. Learn to recognize <u>your</u> signs so that you know when the chakra is completely cleansed. Often times, this chakra is cleansed much quicker than the time taken to cleanse the body chakras.

30. Once the cleansing of the Star Chakra is complete, ask the Angels to assist in infusing the Star Chakra with the "Rays of Light" and to completely fill this chakra with the frequencies of love, remembrance, and "all that is," which are perfect for the recipient at this time. Hold your hands, palms facing down, hovering over the Star Chakra, and infuse the frequencies of the "Rays of Light" coming through your palms into the recipient's chakra. Cup your hands on either side of the cone that you are visualizing. Use your intentions to visualize the "Rays of Light" streaming through your palms to the chakra.

31. Pay very close attention to any messages or images that you receive during this time. This information is to be shared with the recipient once the session is complete. Also pay close attention to the *feel* of these frequencies as the infusing of the "Rays of Light" is taking place. Learn how these frequencies feel to you as they fill this chakra with *love*. You will *feel* or notice the frequencies in different ways; however, you will notice a gentle pressure pushing up on your palms from the Star Chakra, when the chakra is full. You do not want to over fill the chakra. You may also ask the Angels to please *let you know* when the chakra is full. Learn to recognize <u>your</u> signs so that you know when the chakra is full.

32. Once you notice the distinct pressure on your palms indicating that the chakra is full, keeping your palms facing down, gently and slowly move your palms higher, stopping at intervals to notice the pressure to make sure that the pressure is also continuing upward. When you are feeling that pressure and your hands are following your movement upward, move your palms high enough so that they are close to the level of your eyes. If it is more comfortable to stop a little lower, that is fine. Continue to extend your palms straight out in front of you, across from your eyes, turn your palms facing upward and gently wave them across the top of the pressure coming from the chakra, at that level. This will seal the chakra and allow you to move your intentions on to the next chakra.

33. Next, hold your hands directly over the recipient's Stargate Chakra, shaping your hands around the visualization of the middle of a cone, and above the recipient's Crown Chakra. Notice that this chakra is different than the other chakras. It is swirling in a cone shape above the Crown Chakra, with the swirling motion of the energy interlocking with the Star Chakra. The cone is facing upward and away from the Crown Chakra.

34. Ask the Angels for assistance cleansing out the Stargate Chakra completely; ask for assistance in removing all energy that is not of a high vibration. Visualize what it might look like as the energy is being removed from the chakra. Move your hands back and forth, in a semi-

circular motion, surrounding this Stargate Chakra as the cleansing is taking place. This motion will assist in releasing any unwanted energy. Pay very close attention to any messages or images that you receive during this time. This information is to be shared with the recipient after the session is complete. Also pay close attention to the *feel* of the energy as the cleansing is taking place. Learn how this energy feels to you. You will *feel* or notice the energy in different ways; it can be swirling, hot, cold, or pressure, etc. You may ask the Angels to please *let you know* (give you a sign) when the cleansing is complete. You may also *feel* when the activity of the energy surrounding the chakra has stopped, letting you know that it is complete. Learn to recognize your signs so that you know when the chakra is completely cleansed. Often times, this chakra is cleansed much quicker than the time taken to cleanse the body chakras.

35. Once the cleansing of the Stargate chakra is complete, ask the Angels to assist in infusing the Stargate Chakra with the "Rays of Light" and to completely fill this chakra with the frequencies of love, remembrance, and "all that is," which are perfect for the recipient at this time. Hold your hands, palms facing down, hovering over the Stargate chakra, and infuse the frequencies of the "Rays of Light" coming through your palms into the recipient's chakra. Cup your hands on either side of the cone that you are visualizing. Use your intentions and visualize the

"Rays of Light" streaming through your palms into the chakra.

36. Pay very close attention to any messages or images that you receive during this time. This information is to be shared with the recipient once the session is complete. Also pay close attention to the *feel* of these frequencies as the infusing of the "Rays of Light" is taking place. Learn how these frequencies feel to you as they fill this chakra with *love*. You will *feel* or notice these frequencies in different ways; however, you will notice a gentle pressure pushing up on your palms, from the Stargate Chakra, when the chakra is full. You do not want to over fill the chakra. You may also ask the Angels to please *let you know* when the chakra is full. Learn to recognize your signs so that you know when the chakra is full.

37. Once you notice the distinct pressure on your palms indicating that the chakra is full, keeping your palms facing down, gently and slowly move your palms higher, stopping at intervals to notice the pressure to make sure that the pressure is also continuing upward. When you are feeling that pressure and your hands are following your movement upward, move your palms high enough so that they are close to the level of your eyes. If it is more comfortable to stop a little lower, that is fine. Continue to extend your palms straight out in front of you, across from your eyes, turn your palms facing upward and gently wave them across the top of the

pressure coming from the chakra, at that level. This will seal the chakra and allow you to move your intentions on to the next chakra.

38. Next, hold your hands directly over the recipient's Supernova Chakra, shaping your hands around the visualization of the upper end of the cone, and above the recipient's Crown Chakra. Notice that this chakra is different than all of the other chakras (including the Star and the Stargate Chakras). It is swirling on the outside of the cone shape, above the Star and Stargate Chakras, weaving downward towards the point of the cone.

39. Ask the Angels for assistance in cleansing out the Supernova Chakra completely; ask for assistance in removing all energy that is not of a high vibration. Visualize what it might look like as the energy is being removed from the chakra. Move your hands back and forth, in a semi-circular motion, surrounding this Supernova Chakra as the cleansing is taking place. This motion will assist releasing any unwanted energy. Pay very close attention to any messages or images that you receive during this time. This information is to be shared with the recipient after the session is complete. Also pay close attention to the *feel* of the energy as the cleansing is taking place. Learn how this energy feels to you. You will *feel* or notice the energy in different ways; it can be swirling, hot, cold, or pressure, etc. You may ask the Angels to please *let you know* (give you a sign) when the cleansing is complete. You may also *feel* when

the activity of the energy surrounding the chakra has stopped, letting you know that it is complete. Learn to recognize your signs so that you know when the chakra is completely cleansed. Often times, this chakra is cleansed much quicker than the time taken to cleanse the body chakras.

40. Once the cleansing of the Supernova Chakra is complete, ask the Angels to assist in infusing the Supernova Chakra with the "Rays of Light" and to completely fill this chakra with the frequencies of love, remembrance, and "all that is," which are perfect for the recipient at this time. Hold your hands, palms facing down, hovering over the Supernova Chakra, and infuse the frequencies of the "Rays of Light" coming through your palms into the recipient's chakra. Cup your hands on either side of the cone that you are visualizing. Use your intentions to visualize the "Rays of Light" streaming through your palms into the chakra.

41. Pay very close attention to any messages or images that you receive during this time. This information is to be shared with the recipient once the healing session is complete. Also pay close attention to the *feel* of these frequencies as the infusing of the "Rays of Light" is taking place. Learn how these frequencies feel to you as they fill this chakra with *love*. You will *feel* or notice the frequencies in different ways; however, you will notice a gentle pressure pushing up on your palms, from the Supernova Chakra, when the chakra is full. You do not

want to over fill the chakra. You may also ask the Angels to please *let you know* when the chakra is full. Learn to recognize your signs so that you know when the chakra is full.

42. Once you notice the distinct pressure on your palms indicating that the chakra is full, keeping your palms facing down, gently and slowly move your palms higher, stopping at intervals to notice the pressure to make sure that the pressure is also continuing upward. When you are feeling that pressure and your hands are following your movement upward, move your palms high enough so that they are close to the level of your eyes. If it is more comfortable to stop a little lower, that is fine. Continue to extend your palms straight out in front of you, across from your eyes, turn your palms facing upward and gently wave them across the top of the pressure coming from the chakra, at that level. This will seal the chakra and allow you to move your intentions on to the next chakra.

43. Hold both of your hands above the recipient's Heart Chakra; use a sweeping motion to sweep away the energies and frequencies from the Heart Chakra up past the Supernova Chakra, eight separate times. This sweeping motion is aligning the chakras.

44. Next, cup your hands into a circle hovering directly over the Solar Plexus Chakra, without touching the skin or clothing of the recipient. If you are touching the recipient's skin or clothing, you may not *feel* the energy

of the cleansing, but rather, you may be feeling the sensations of the recipient's skin or clothing. When you hover, you tend to feel only energy.

45. Ask the Angels for assistance in cleansing out the Solar Plexus Chakra completely; ask the Angels to assist in removing all energy that is not of a high vibration. Visualize what it might look like as the energy is being removed from the chakra. Pay very close attention to any messages or images that you receive during this time. This information is to be shared with the recipient after the session is complete. Also pay close attention to the *feel* of the energy as the cleansing is taking place. Learn how this energy feels to you. You will *feel* or notice the energy in different ways; it can be swirling, hot, cold, or pressure, etc. You may ask the Angels to please *let you know* (give you a sign) when the cleansing is complete. You may also *feel* when the activity of the energy surrounding the chakra has stopped, letting you know that it is complete. Learn to recognize your signs so that you know when the chakra is completely cleansed.

46. Once the cleansing of the Solar Plexus Chakra is complete, ask the Angels to assist in infusing the Solar Plexus Chakra with the "Rays of Light" and to completely fill this chakra with the frequencies of love, remembrance, and "all that is," which are perfect for the recipient at this time. Hold your hands, palms facing down, hovering over the Solar Plexus Chakra, again

without touching the skin or clothing of the recipient, and infuse the frequencies of the "Rays of Light" coming through your palms into the recipient's chakra. Use your intentions and visualize the "Rays of Light" streaming through your palms into the chakra.

47. Pay very close attention to any messages or images that you receive during this time. This information is to be shared with the recipient once the healing session is complete. Also pay close attention to the *feel* of these frequencies as the infusing of the "Rays of Light" is taking place. Learn how these frequencies feel to you as they fill this chakra with *love*. You will *feel* or notice the frequencies in different ways; however, you will notice a gentle pressure pushing up on your palms, from the Solar Plexus Chakra, when the chakra is full. You do not want to overfill the chakra. You may also ask the Angels to please *let you know* when the chakra is full. Learn to recognize <u>your</u> signs so that you know when the chakra is full.

48. Once you notice the distinct pressure on your palms indicating that the chakra is full, keeping your palms facing down, gently and slowly move your palms higher, stopping at intervals to notice the pressure to make sure that the pressure is also continuing upward. When you are feeling that pressure and your hands are following your movement upward, move your palms high enough so that they are close to the level of your eyes. If it is more comfortable to stop a little lower, that is fine.

Continue to extend your palms straight out in front of you, across from your eyes, turn your palms facing upward and gently wave them across the top of the pressure coming from the chakra, at that level. This will seal the chakra and allow you to move your intentions on to the next chakra.

49. Next, cup your hands into a circle hovering directly over the <u>Sacral Chakra</u>, without touching the skin or clothing of the recipient. If you are touching the recipient's skin or clothing, you may not *feel* the energy of the cleansing, but rather, you may be feeling the sensations of the recipient's skin or clothing. When you hover, you tend to feel only energy.

50. Ask the Angels for assistance in cleansing out the Sacral Chakra completely; ask the Angels to assist in removing all energy that is not of a high vibration. Visualize what it might look like as the energy is being removed from the chakra. Pay very close attention to any messages or images that you receive during this time. This information is to be shared with the recipient after the healing session is complete. Also pay close attention to the *feel* of the energy as the cleansing is taking place. Learn how this energy feels to you. You will *feel* or notice the energy in different ways; it can be swirling, hot, cold, or pressure, etc. You may ask the Angels to please *let you know* (give you a sign) when the cleansing is complete. You may also *feel* when the activity of the energy surrounding the chakra has stopped, letting you

know that it is complete. Learn to recognize <u>your</u> signs so that you know when that the chakra is completely cleansed.

51. Once the cleansing of the Sacral Chakra is complete, ask the Angels to assist in infusing the Sacral Chakra with the "Rays of Light" and to completely fill this chakra with the frequencies of love, remembrance, and "all that is," which are perfect for the recipient at this time. Hold your hands, palms facing down, hovering over the Sacral Chakra, again without touching the skin or clothing of the recipient, and infuse the frequencies of the "Rays of Light" that are coming through your palms into the recipient's chakra. Use your intentions and visualize the "Rays of Light" streaming through your palms into the chakra.

52. Pay very close attention to any messages or images that you receive during this time. This information is to be shared with the recipient once the session is complete. Also pay close attention to the *feel* of these frequencies as the infusing of the "Rays of Light" is taking place. Learn how these frequencies feel to you as they fill this chakra with *love*. You will *feel* or notice the frequencies in different ways; however, you will notice a gentle pressure pushing up on your palms, from the Sacral Chakra, when the chakra is full. You do not want to overfill the chakra. You may also ask the Angels to please *let you know* when the chakra is full. Learn to

recognize <u>your</u> signs so that you know when the chakra is full.

53. Once you notice the distinct pressure on your palms indicating that the chakra is full, keeping your palms facing down, gently and slowly move your palms higher, stopping at intervals to notice the pressure to make sure that the pressure is also continuing upward. When you are feeling that pressure and your hands are following your movement upward, move your palms high enough so that they are close to the level of your eyes. If it is more comfortable to stop a little lower, that is fine. Continue to extend your palms straight out in front of you, across from your eyes, turn your palms facing upward and gently wave them across the top of the pressure coming from the chakra, at that level. This will seal the chakra and allow you to move your intentions on to the next chakra.

54. Next, cup your hands into a circle hovering directly over the <u>Base Chakra</u>, without touching the skin or clothing of the recipient. If you are touching the recipient's skin or clothing, you may not *feel* the energy of the cleansing, but rather, you may be feeling the sensations of the recipient's skin or clothing. When you hover, you tend to feel only energy.

55. Ask the Angels for assistance in cleansing out the Base Chakra completely; ask the Angels for assistance in removing all energy that is not of a high vibration. Visualize what it might look like as the energy is being

removed from the chakra. Pay very close attention to any messages or images that you receive during this time. This information is to be shared with the recipient after the session is complete. Also pay close attention to the *feel* of the energy as the cleansing is taking place. Learn how this energy feels to you. You will *feel* or notice the energy in different ways; it can be swirling, hot, cold, or pressure, etc. You may ask the Angels to please *let you know* (give you a sign) when the cleansing is complete. You may also *feel* when the activity of the energy surrounding the chakra has stopped, letting you know that it is complete. Learn to recognize your signs so that you know when that the chakra is completely cleansed.

56. Once the cleansing of the Base Chakra is complete, ask the Angels to assist in infusing the Base Chakra with the "Rays of Light" and to completely fill this chakra with the frequencies of love, remembrance, and "all that is," which are perfect for the recipient at this time. Hold your hands, palms facing down, hovering over the Base Chakra, again without touching the skin or clothing of the recipient, and infuse the frequencies of the "Rays of Light" that are coming through your palms into the recipient's chakra. Use your intentions and visualize the "Rays of Light" streaming through your palms into the chakra.

57. Pay very close attention to any messages or images that you receive during this time (This information is to

be shared with the recipient once the session is complete.) Also pay close attention to the *feel* of these frequencies as the infusing of the "Rays of Light" is taking place. Learn how these frequencies feel to you as they fill this chakra with *love*. You will *feel* or notice the frequencies in different ways; however, you will notice a gentle pressure pushing up on your palms, from the Base Chakra, when the chakra is full. You do not want to over fill the chakra. You may also ask the Angels to please *let you know* when the chakra is full. Learn to recognize your signs so that you know when the chakra is full.

58. Once you notice the distinct pressure on your palms indicating that the chakra is full, keeping your palms facing down, gently and slowly move your palms higher, stopping at intervals to notice the pressure to make sure that the pressure is also continuing upward. When you are feeling that pressure and your hands are following your movement upward, move your palms high enough so that they are close to the level of your eyes. If it is more comfortable to stop a little lower, that is fine. Continue to extend your palms straight out in front of you, across from your eyes, turn your palms facing upward and gently wave them across the top of the pressure coming from the chakra, at that level. This will seal the chakra and allow you to move your intentions on to the next chakra.

59. Next, cup your hands into a circle hovering directly over the Root Chakra, without touching the skin or

clothing of the recipient. If you are touching the recipient's skin or clothing, you may not *feel* the energy of the cleansing, but rather, you may be feeling the sensations of the recipient's skin or clothing. When you hover, you tend to feel only energy.

60. Ask the Angels for assistance in cleansing out the Root Chakra completely; ask the Angels for assistance in removing all energy that is not of a high vibration. Visualize what it might look like as the energy is being removed from the chakra. Pay very close attention to any messages or images that you receive during this time. This information is to be shared with the recipient after the healing session is complete. Also pay close attention to the *feel* of the energy as the cleansing is taking place. Learn how this energy feels to you. You will *feel* or notice the energy in different ways; it can be swirling, hot, cold, or pressure, etc. You may ask the Angels to please let you know (give you a sign) when the cleansing is complete. You may also *feel* when the activity of the energy surrounding the chakra has stopped, letting you know that it is complete. Learn to recognize your signs so that you know when the chakra is completely cleansed.

61. Once the cleansing of the Root Chakra is complete, ask the Angels to assist in infusing the Root Chakra with the "Rays of Light" and to completely fill this chakra with the frequencies of love, remembrance, and "all that is," which are perfect for the recipient at this time. Hold

your hands, palms facing down, hovering over the Root Chakra, again without touching the skin or clothing of the recipient, and infuse the frequencies of the "Rays of Light" coming through your palms into the recipient's chakra. Use your intentions and visualize the "Rays of Light" streaming through your palms into the chakra.

62. Pay very close attention to any messages or images that you receive during this time. This information is to be shared with the recipient once the session is complete. Also pay close attention to the *feel* of these frequencies as the infusing of the "Rays of Light" is taking place. Learn how these frequencies feel to you as they fill this chakra with *love*. You will *feel* or notice the frequencies in different ways; however, you will notice a gentle pressure pushing up on your palms, from the Root Chakra, when the chakra is full. You do not want to over fill the chakra. You may also ask the Angels to please *let you know* when the chakra is full. Learn to recognize your signs so that you know when the chakra is full.

63. Once you notice the distinct pressure on your palms indicating that the chakra is full, keeping your palms facing down, gently and slowly move your palms higher, stopping at intervals to notice the pressure to make sure that the pressure is also continuing upward. When you are feeling that pressure and your hands are following your movement upward, move your palms high enough so that they are close to the level of your eyes. If it is more comfortable to stop a little lower, that is fine.

Continue to extend your palms straight out in front of you, across from your eyes, turn your palms facing upward and gently wave them across the top of the pressure coming from the chakra, at that level. This will seal the chakra and allow you to move your intentions on to the next chakra.

64. Next, cup your hands into a circle hovering directly over the Earth Star Chakra.

65. Ask the Angels for assistance in cleansing out the Earth Star Chakra completely; ask the Angels for assistance in removing all energy that is not of a high vibration. Move your hands back and forth, in a circular motion (as if you are rubbing the outside of a ball,) surrounding this Earth Star Chakra as the cleansing is taking place. This motion will assist in releasing any unwanted energy. Visualize what it might look like as the energy is being removed from the chakra. Pay very close attention to any messages or images that you receive during this time. This information is to be shared with the recipient after the healing session is complete. Also pay close attention to the *feel* of the energy as the cleansing is taking place. Learn how this energy feels to you. You will *feel* or notice the energy in different ways; it can be swirling, hot, cold, or pressure, etc. You may ask the Angels to please *let you know* (give you a sign) when the cleansing is complete. You may also *feel* when the activity of the energy surrounding the chakra has stopped, letting you know that it is complete. Learn to recognize your signs

so that you know when the chakra is completely cleansed.

66. Once the cleansing of the Earth Star Chakra is complete, ask the Angels to assist in infusing the Earth Star Chakra with the "Rays of Light" and to completely fill this chakra with the frequencies of love, remembrance, and "all that is," which are perfect for the recipient at this time. Hold your hands, palms facing down, hovering over the Earth Star Chakra, and infuse the frequencies of the "Rays of Light" that are coming through your palms into the recipient's chakra. Use your intentions and visualize the "Rays of Light" streaming through your palms into the chakra.

84. Pay very close attention to any messages or images that you receive during this time. This information is to be shared with the recipient once the session is complete. Also pay close attention to the *feel* of these frequencies as the infusing of the "Rays of Light" is taking place. Learn how these frequencies feel to you as they fill this chakra with *love*. You will *feel* or notice the frequencies in different ways; however, you will notice a gentle pressure pushing up on your palms, from the Earth Star Chakra, when the chakra is full. You do not want to overfill the chakra. You may also ask the Angels to please *let you know* when the chakra is full. Learn to recognize <u>your</u> signs so that you know when the chakra is full.

67. Once you notice the distinct pressure on your palms indicating that the chakra is full, keeping your palms facing down, gently and slowly move your palms higher, stopping at intervals to notice the pressure to make sure that the pressure is also continuing upward. When you are feeling that pressure and your hands are following your movement upward, move your palms high enough so that they are close to the level of your eyes. If it is more comfortable to stop a little lower, that is fine. Continue to extend your palms straight out in front of you, across from your eyes, turn your palms facing upward and gently wave them across the top of the pressure coming from the chakra, at that level. This will seal the chakra and allow you to move your intentions on to the next chakra.

68. Next, cup your hands into a circle hovering directly over the Earth Heart Chakra.

69. Ask the Angels for assistance in cleansing out the Earth Heart Chakra completely; ask the Angels for assistance in removing all energy that is not of a high vibration. Move your hands back and forth, in a circular motion (as if you are rubbing the outside of a ball), surrounding this Earth Heart Chakra as the cleansing is taking place. This motion will assist in releasing any unwanted energy. Visualize what it might look like as the energy is being removed from the chakra. Pay very close attention to any messages or images that you receive during this time. This information is to be shared with the recipient

after the healing session is complete. Also pay close attention to the *feel* of the energy as the cleansing is taking place. Learn how this energy feels to you. You will *feel* or notice the energy in different ways; it can be swirling, hot, cold, or pressure, etc. You may ask the Angels to please *let you know* (give you a sign) when the cleansing is complete. You may also *feel* when the activity of the energy surrounding the chakra has stopped, letting you know that it is complete. Learn to recognize your signs so that you know when that the chakra is completely cleansed.

70. Once the cleansing of the Earth Heart Chakra is complete, ask the Angels to assist in infusing the Earth Heart Chakra with the "Rays of Light" and to completely fill this chakra with the frequencies of love, remembrance, and "all that is," which are perfect for the recipient at this time. Hold your hands, palms facing down, hovering over the Earth Heart Chakra, and infuse the frequencies of the "Rays of Light" that are coming through your palms into the recipient's chakra. Use your intentions and visualize the "Rays of Light" streaming through your palms into the chakra.

71. Pay very close attention to any messages or images that you receive during this time. This information is to be shared with the recipient once the session is complete. Also pay close attention to the *feel* of these frequencies as the infusing of the "Rays of Light" is taking place. Learn how these frequencies feel to you as

they fill this chakra with *love*. You will *feel* or notice the frequencies in different ways; however, you will notice a gentle pressure pushing up on your palms, from the Earth Heart Chakra, when the chakra is full. You do not want to overfill the chakra. You may also ask the Angels to please *let you know* when the chakra is full. Learn to recognize your signs so that you know when the chakra is full.

72. Once you notice the distinct pressure on your palms indicating that the chakra is full, keeping your palms facing down, gently and slowly move your palms higher, stopping at intervals to notice the pressure to make sure that the pressure is also continuing upward. When you are feeling that pressure and your hands are following your movement upward, move your palms high enough so that they are close to the level of your eyes. If it is more comfortable to stop a little lower, that is fine. Continue to extend your palms straight out in front of you, across from your eyes, turn your palms facing upward and gently wave them across the top of the pressure coming from the chakra, at that level. This will seal the chakra and allow you to move your intentions on to the next chakra.

73. Hold both of your hands above the recipient's Heart Chakra; use a sweeping motion to sweep away the energies and frequencies from the Heart Chakra down past the Earth Heart Chakra, eight separate times. This sweeping motion is aligning the chakras.

74. Step to the feet of the recipient, facing your open palms toward the bottoms of their feet. Ask for the frequencies of the "Rays of Light" to fill the recipient's entire body, cleansing, healing, balancing, and re-aligning all of their chakras, every cell in their body, and their aura, in the physical and non-physical, on all levels and in all time and space. Stay in this position for a minute or two until you feel that this is complete.

75. Step to the head of the recipient, facing your open palms toward their Crown Chakra. Ask for the frequencies of the "Rays of Light" to fill the recipient's entire body, cleansing, healing, balancing, and re-aligning all of their chakras, every cell in their body, and their aura, in the physical and non-physical, on all levels and in all time and space. Stay in this position for a minute or two until you feel that this is complete.

76. Once you feel a completion, place your palms at the bottom of the recipient's feet. Sweep your palms over the recipient to the top of their Crown Chakra, surrounding them in a cocoon filled with protective frequencies and energies. The session is complete.

77. Give gratitude to your Divine Source, the Angels (especially Archangel Michael and Archangel Gabrielle,) and your guides, the recipient's Angels and guides, your higher self, and the recipient's higher self, Mother Earth, any other being from the Divine realm, and all loving

beings of the "Rays of Light" who have assisted you in this session.

78. Ask how the recipient feels, allowing them to slowly sit up when they are feeling grounded. Provide water for them, if they wish to assist in their grounding. Water can assist if the recipient feels light headed or disoriented. When they are comfortable enough, you can both sit back into your chairs so that you can hear about the recipient's experience and you can share the messages and information with the recipient that you received during the session. This session's discussion is brief compared to the Healing Session as it is basically cleaning, balancing, and re-aligning the chakras for someone that has already received a full Healing Session is complete.

79. Remind the recipient to continue to use their affirmations and create new affirmations, using their index cards, when it feels right to do so. Also remind the recipient to be very mindful of their vibrations attached to their emotions in their creations. Remind them *how it works* as you now know yourself from reading this information.

Conclusion
What next?

<u>Conclusion: What Next?</u>

This information is intended to introduce you to the "Rays of Light" and their teachings. It is meant to bring to your attention that the rays are available and they are for everyone. The information is shared to provide various examples of how the "Rays of Light" can be accessed and used. If you were born into a physical body on this earth, you can access the "Rays of Light" to assist you in any way that you wish to create, or to *un-create*, so to speak, by releasing old patterns and low vibrating emotions.

Not all the answers are provided in this book, nor was that the intention. The intention is to provide information and to create a thirst for more by prompting questions. It is meant to provide a healthy approach to assist you in your journey of experience and enjoyment of life and to bring happiness on a daily basis. It is meant to remind you that you and only you create your day.

This book provides thoughts, ideas, perspectives, and information to sharpen your beautiful tools, for you to test, to experiment, and to adjust what works for you in order to bring about what you desire. This book adds new ideas and suggestion that are simple and effective to assist you in creating a new reference and a new point of view. It is your choice to determine if the ideas feel right to you. It is through attraction that each of you chooses what feels right. The simple fact that you are reading this book indicates your interest in something written within these pages. It will be your choice if you decide to experiment, to test out the ideas or practices, and to decide what works, and what feels right for you.

The word *healing* is used in the title '"Rays of Light" – A Healing Modality."' The word *healing* is used in a general way, by the definition in this book, referring to your personal growth and changes that you make in choosing to create a good feeling, an experience of high vibrating emotions such a love, or in experiencing a physical change in your body (on all levels) that feels more comfortable to you. The word *healing* is not used in the same way that a doctor may understand or use the word. This is a new way of seeing this word, *healing* from a different perspective.

The "Rays of Light" and their frequencies, the Divine Source (however you experience that) and the Angels are for everyone, no exceptions. Everyone has access to the "Rays of Light." You need only ask and be open to receiving. You do not need permission, you do not need to take a class, nor do you need to be activated, receive certification, or an attunement. Since you were born on this earth, your body has been attuned. There are no requirements; you are ready to receive. You were born deserving of receiving. There is no limit as to how much you can receive or to how often you can ask for assistance. The more you receive the frequencies and energies, the greater the result. The greater the result, the more you understand and remember the truths, allowing you to let go of the myths of old patterns that you were taught. As you remember your truths you are living the freedom that you possess.

The following simple prayer is recommended for daily use to assist you with healthy protection and to bring bursts of love into your everyday life. This is protection for what you can see and what you cannot see. This prayer is not to be used with the vibrations of fear or concern (as you know they would carry low vibrating emotions), but to be used with trust and belief and most of all with love, which carry emotions with the highest of vibrations. Believe and trust that all you need do is to ask and you are safe. Believe and trust that all you need do is to ask and you are protected. Believe and trust. That is all you need to do. Ask and you have a loving being by your side, waiting to attend to your every desire. Ask and know that you could never be alone, as you <u>are</u> Divine, and you <u>are</u> love.

Prayer of Love and Protection

I ask all loving beings of the "Rays of Light" to surround me with a veil of love and protection, in the physical and non-physical, on all levels and in all time and space. I ask for this veil to allow only the highest of vibrations, releasing all else, with love, grace and gratitude.

A final note from the author, Linda:

I wish to thank each of you for your time, in allowing me the honor of sharing this information and these beautiful teachings. May your days be filled with the freedoms of love, joy, and, abundance in life.

With Love,

Linda Street

Made in the USA
Charleston, SC
15 May 2014